WILLIAM PENN
Architect of a Nation

❖

John B. B. Trussell

Commonwealth of Pennsylvania
Pennsylvania Historical and Museum Commission
Harrisburg, 1998

COMMONWEALTH OF PENNSYLVANIA

Tom Ridge
Governor

THE PENNSYLVANIA HISTORICAL
AND MUSEUM COMMISSION

Janet S. Klein, *Chairman*

William A. Cornell, *Vice Chairman*

James M. Adovasio

Thomas C. Corrigan, *Representative*

Edwin G. Holl, *Senator*

Nancy D. Kolb

John W. Lawrence, M.D.

Stephen R. Maitland, *Representative*

George A. Nichols

LeRoy Patrick

Allyson Y. Schwartz, *Senator*

Eugene W. Hickok, *Secretary of Education, ex officio*

❖

Brent D. Glass
Executive Director

Fifth Printing
Copyright © 1980 Commonwealth of Pennsylvania
ISBN 0-89271-008-X

Acknowledgments

This booklet about William Penn has been prepared with the purpose of making more widely known the life and work of the founder of Pennsylvania, especially in the Commonwealth which he established three hundred years ago. Its publication is a contribution of the Pennsylvania Historical and Museum Commission to the State-wide observance of the anniversary of that founding, which William Penn envisioned in 1681 as a fresh start in the social and political life of man. The members of the Commission have incurred the gratitude of the author for the approval and support that they gave to this undertaking. Appreciation for the same support and encouragement must also be expressed to William J. Wewer, Executive Director of the Commission; to Harry E. Whipkey, Director of the Bureau of Archives and History; to John Bodnar, Chief of the Division of History, who supervised publication; to Harold L. Myers, Associate Historian, who was responsible for publication; and to Mrs. Roxane Kauffman, who assisted with the proof. This manuscript had also the benefit of the critical judgment of three authorities, Edwin B. Bronner, professor of history and Librarian, Haverford College; Richard S. Dunn, professor of history, the University of Pennsylvania; and William A. Hunter, former chief of the Division of History.

In this Pennsylvania State Capitol mural, the painter, Violet Oakley, celebrated William Penn's determination, in her words, to "bring out of captivity all those who were oppressed for conscience' sake."

WILLIAM PENN
Architect of a Nation

Introduction

WILLIAM Penn is chiefly remembered as the first Proprietor of Pennsylvania and a leading member of the Society of Friends. Less frequently recognized is the tremendous influence, indirect as well as direct, that he exerted on the evolution not only of Pennsylvania but of America as a whole. The concepts he advanced and the practices he sought to establish represent many of the principles which, although widely considered radical in his own day, are accepted now as typifying some of the most fundamental elements of the American philosophy: he welcomed to his Province people of all national backgrounds; he promoted the principle of popular self-government; above all, he insisted on a degree of freedom of religion which existed almost nowhere else in the world. The result was that Pennsylvania early drew immigrants from a diversity of countries, bringing with them a variety of skills and occupations. Almost from the beginning its society became more cosmopolitan and its economy developed along more complex lines than was the case for the predominantly agricultural and ethnically more homogeneous colonies comprising the rest of British America. In a number of important respects, the patterns which the country as a whole would eventually follow were initiated in Pennsylvania.

Background

Considering the characteristics for which Penn is remembered, his background could hardly be more incongruous. He was an advocate of non-violence, a passionate believer in human equality, a non-conformist in religion to the point that he went to prison rather than compromise his beliefs. His father, also named William, represented sharply contrasting viewpoints. He became a national hero for his naval exploits in a succession of wars; he was an admiral schooled in the tradition of an authoritarian system, a knight who aspired to an earldom; he was a man who, during an age of theological and sectarian disputation, took little interest in religion and accepted without question the tenets of the Established Church.

Nevertheless, it is true that in a not inconsiderable way the father deserves to share with the son the credit for the establishment of Pennsylvania. It was for him, in fact, and not his son, that the new Province was named — and at the express insistence of King Charles II. Moreover, the grant of the land in the first place was made as acknowledgement by the King of an obligation to the Admiral's memory — a debt of gratitude and affection as well as of money. Beyond that, lasting appreciation of the services of Admiral Penn was an important factor in fending off a number of the moves which occurred over several years to deprive the younger William Penn of his proprietorship of Pennsylvania.

That William Penn, who was born at London on October 14, 1644 (Old Style), was christened with the name borne by almost all the men in his direct line for as far back as his ancestry has been authoritatively documented. Although he claimed kinship with a previously more prominent Penn family of Buckinghamshire (a claim reciprocated by the Buckinghamshire Penns), the actual connection has not been established. What is known is that a William Penn, the great-great-grandfather of the Proprietor, was a prosperous yeoman of Minety, Gloucestershire, and was buried there following his death in 1591. His son, a second William, was a law clerk. In a break with the tradition, the son representing the next generation in the Proprietor's line was named Giles; he became a sea captain and merchant, serving for some years as the English consul at Salé, in Morocco. It was Giles's son, a third William, who became the admiral. This William Penn, having been trained for the sea, captained one of his father's ships on merchant voyages, principally to the Mediterranean. Events, however, would soon give his career a permanent, new direction.

Late in 1641, Catholics in Ireland began uprisings against the Protestant Anglo-Irish who had dispossessed them of their lands. The following summer, long-smoldering disputes between Parliament and King Charles I broke out into open civil war, and the insurgents in Ireland swung their backing to the King. One of the responses of the Parliamentary leaders was to set about creating a navy to patrol the Irish seas to limit contact between the Royalists in England and their supporters in Ireland.

A newly forming navy had a crying need for experienced seamen. Although William Penn was only twenty-one years old, when he entered the Parliament's naval service he was almost immediately given command of one of the ships in the squadron beating back and forth along the Irish coast. He rapidly distinguished himself,

Admiral Sir William Penn, father of the founder of Pennsylvania, painted by Sir Peter Lely (courtesy, National Maritime Museum, London).

capturing not only Royalist vessels but also ships trying to bring supplies and reinforcements from Catholic countries on the European continent, and taking part in what would now be called commando operations against Royalist towns and strongholds on the Irish mainland.

Briefly in London in 1643, on June 6 he was married to a young widow, Margaret Jasper Vanderschuren, whose family had been among the Protestant refugees fleeing Ireland because of the uprisings and the massacres which followed. He was again in England at the time of the birth of his first son, another William, in October, 1644. Immediately after the baby's baptism on October 23, however, he put to sea once more for over a year of further successes which led to his promotion to Rear Admiral.

By that time the phase of the conflict known as the "First Civil War" was coming to an end. The King was in Parliament's custody, but political realignments were taking place. Some of the leaders of the Parliamentary forces were disturbed at the indications that power was being centralized in the hands of Oliver Cromwell. A second civil war was in the making, plotting was rife, and defection of military and naval forces was feared. The young admiral was one of those who came under suspicion, and in 1648 he was briefly imprisoned. Aside from the possibility of treasonable activities, there were allegations that he had cheated his crews out of their fair share of prize money, but the issue was soon dropped and he was restored to his command. Before leaving for sea service once more, however, he moved his family to Wanstead, in Essex, some ten miles outside of London.

The execution of Charles I in January, 1649 horrified many but ended the resistance in England for the time being, leaving Cromwell free to turn his full attention to the subjection of Ireland. Admiral Penn was actively involved in supporting this campaign. Then, promoted to vice admiral, he sailed his fleet into the Mediterranean in pursuit of remnants of the Royalist forces. Within a matter of months, England was at war with the Dutch, with Admiral Penn winning further laurels in naval battles in September, 1652, again in February, 1653, and in the war's final engagements in June and July.

These achievements brought his elevation to the Navy Commission, the body that exercised both the administrative and the tactical direction of the fleet. Being stationed in London also gave him the opportunity to pursue successfully a petition for a grant of land confiscated from Royalists in Ireland, his claim being based on the losses—property yielding three hundred pounds a year in rents—that his wife had suffered due to the uprisings. The grant, an estate near Cork called Macroom, was approved, in part as restitution to Margaret Penn and in part as recognition for the Admiral's services. With it, he was awarded a gold chain and medal worth a hundred pounds.

But a change of fortune was in the offing. Late in 1654, Admiral Penn (with the added title of "General at Sea") was put in command of an expedition being sent to capture Hispaniola. The assault failed and, rather than return to England empty handed, Penn on his own authority sailed to Jamaica and captured that island. But if he had thought to appease Oliver Cromwell, he was disappointed, for both he and Gen. Robert Venables, commander of the expedition's contingent of soldiers, were imprisoned in the Tower of London on grounds that are still not clear but may have been suspicion of treason. Whatever the case, he was released after five weeks, but was retired from the navy. Both to avoid attracting official attention and to see to his properties, in August, 1656 he moved with his family to Ireland to live on his Macroom estate.

As for the eleven-year-old William, the move brought an end to what had been the first of what by modern standards were to be, altogether, very limited associations with formal academic education. Until less than a year earlier, when he entered Chigwell Free Grammar School, near Wanstead, his education had been carried out at home. For the next four years his schooling would depend on private tutoring augmented by his own reading.

This was probably extensive, for by all accounts he was a studious, serious, bookish boy, markedly contrasting in temperament with his bluff, hearty, extroverted father. Because theology dominated intellectual activity in that era, religious thought would have occupied a major place in his reading, with a consequently significant influence on his development. At the same time, during the years when he was growing up in Ireland, he does not appear to have displayed any exceptional degree of piety or religious activity beyond what was normal for the times. Observance of the forms of religion, at least, was in any case a conspicuous part of everyday life.

William Penn said in later years, however, that it was at this time that he had his first contact with the Quaker sect. In 1657 an itinerant Quaker preacher named Thomas Loe was traveling through the region, and according to Penn's account, the Admiral invited Loe to preach at Macroom. Again according to that account, the Quaker spoke so movingly that Admiral Penn was brought to tears. Nevertheless, while this experience unquestionably had an impact on young William, the effect was residual rather than immediate.

Other matters loomed large in the Penn family's consciousness. The iron dictatorship clamped on Britain by Oliver Cromwell, now proclaimed "Lord Protector," had alienated many. Despite the dangers involved, therefore, contacts with the exiled Royalists on the Continent, led by the son of the martyred King Charles I, who styled himself Charles II, began to be established and extended. Necessarily, these efforts were carried out in great secrecy; records which might be incriminating if discovered were kept to an inescapable minimum. Thus, it has not been possible to document in any detail what role Admiral Penn may have played in this underground activity. That he played an active part and that it was of considerable importance, however, was made evident by subsequent events.

Cromwell's death in October, 1658 was followed by more than a year of political uncertainty and increasing instability. By early 1660 the nation's mood was receptive to a restoration of the Stuart monarchy. A Convention Parliament was called to consider the matter, and Admiral Penn was chosen to sit as a member representing the corporation of Weymouth. Early in April, Parliament agreed to invite Charles II to return as king, and the Admiral was named as a member of the delegation which left at once for Scheveningen, in Holland, to escort the new sovereign back to England. It is significant that almost immediately after the King boarded the ship for the voyage to Dover, Admiral Penn was dubbed knight.

Nor was that the only mark of royal favor shown him. Within weeks, Sir William was appointed as one of the three commissioners of the Royal Navy, under Charles's brother, James, Duke of York, the Lord High Admiral. The one prospective cloud on the horizon was that the Royalist from whom Macroom had been confiscated predictably demanded that his property be returned, but even this resulted to Sir William's advantage: since Macroom had to be given up, the King compensated the Admiral with Shanagarry, a larger estate also not far from Cork which yielded even greater rents. Sir William was also made Governor of the port of Kinsale and captain of its castle and garrison. In monetary terms, his appointments and lands would provide him with what was the impressive income of two thousand pounds a year. His office not only brought him and

Oliver Cromwell, painted by Robert Walker about 1649 (courtesy, National Portrait Gallery, London).

his family back to London but gave him ready access to court, with opportunities for the advancement of his own fortunes—being created Earl of Weymouth did not now seem to be an unattainable goal—and those of his family. For his eldest son, Sir William visualized a career as a courtier which, from the advantageous starting point that had now been provided, could take him to who knew what heights.

Toward a Body of Convictions

As a start on the course the Admiral had charted for him, in October, 1660 William matriculated at Christ Church, Oxford. He entered not as a regular student but as a "gentleman commoner," one of those whose chief purpose was not so much to pursue scholarship as it was to acquire polish and make contacts which could be useful in later life.

William arrived at an Oxford embroiled in controversies due to the efforts of the newly installed Royalist officials of the university to root out practices and individuals associated with the years of Puritan control. Some of the new rulings, such as the requirement for undergraduates to wear a surplice—the symbol of Oxford students' traditional status as prospective candidates for holy orders—and to attend compulsory Church of England chapel provoked student resistance, much of it certainly conscientious but some of it probably no more than the expression of the general rebelliousness of young men enjoying their first taste of relative independence. There is no indication that Penn took any part in the disturbances that occurred. On the contrary, he said later that he had remained aloof from most student activities; he considered that the university was a place of "hellish darkness and debauchery." As for the academic aspects of Oxford, he did not find the emphasis on hair-splitting pedantry which characterized so much of the instruction to be intellectually appealing. He did make some lasting and important friendships, but he put most of his effort into reading widely in the extensive library of his college.

In May, 1661, before the end of Penn's first year at the university, Parliament began passing what would eventually be a total of four laws, known collectively as the Clarendon Code, which sharply restricted the free exercise of religion. The initial law, the Corporation Act, required all municipal officers to participate in the sacraments of the Established Church. This would not have gone unnoticed by a young man of Penn's turn of mind, and when he returned to Oxford for his second year he seems to have been increasingly troubled by the conflict between the direction events were taking and his evolving convictions of what was right. In any case, his dissatisfaction was increased through the association he had established with Dr. John Owen, a noted Puritan theologian who had been dismissed as Vice-Chancellor of the University and Dean of Christ Church when the Royalists regained control. His thinking stimulated by the extracurricular sessions he and other students were attending at Dr. Owen's home, Penn began more and more to question what was being advanced as established dogma.

The attitudes he revealed during a mid-term visit to London in January, 1662 seriously disturbed his father. After William returned to the university, the Admiral began thinking of transferring the young man from Oxford to Cambridge, where he would be removed from Dr. Owen's subversive influence. Whatever action he might have taken was forestalled for, before the end of March, the matter was out of his hands. William returned home, announcing (he later wrote) that he had been "banished" from Oxford by the authorities for having written a book they considered offensive. There is no record of his being expelled, however, and no identification of the reputed book. It is possible that Penn, feeling that he was wasting his time in surroundings he found distasteful, simply dropped out of school. On the other hand, his story that his father had reacted to the news with "whipping, beating and turning out of doors" is readily believable considering Sir William's reputation for a hot temper and his record of impulsive action.

Nevertheless, the "turning out of doors" would clearly have been a temporary measure. Samuel Pepys, the diarist, lived next door to the Penns in London and, as Clerk of the Admiralty, worked in close association with Sir William. In his journal he mentioned that young Penn was living with his parents from March 16 onward. Pepys also noted that relations between the father and son were openly strained.

That May, Parliament passed another law, this one specifically directed at "certain persons called Quakers" who, because of the scruples that prohibited them from taking oaths, had been confused with an extremist, anti-royalist religious group called Fifth Monarchists. This law made it illegal for five or more of them to gather "under pretense of worship." This was followed by the second stage of the Clarendon Code, the Act of Uniformity, which required all clergy to follow without variation the prescribed Prayer Book in the services they conducted. William, who continued to maintain his contact with Dr. Owen through correspondence, became more openly critical of the government's policy of imposing religious conformity. The Admiral clung to the hope that William's attitude merely reflected a passing phase, but there was the risk that before he outgrew it he would do something to embroil himself in official trouble with the authorities. To get the young man out of harm's way, Sir William decided to send him to France, where he might broaden his horizons and acquire some polish at the French court.

Early in July, therefore, William left London for Paris. For some months he led the life of a typical wealthy young Englishman tasting the delights and acquiring the mannerisms and the wardrobe of the world's most elegant capital. Nonetheless, he had not dismissed completely the questions of religion and principle that had been bothering him. And as it happened, a particular experience provided a trigger which, by his own account, influenced the entire course of his life.

What occurred was that, late one evening, a brawl developed when a man he passed on the street announced that Penn had insulted him by refusing to tip his hat in reply to the man's doffing his. In the future, failing to take off his hat was to cause Penn considerable trouble, but this was before he had become a Quaker and the young Englishman explained that he had meant no insult — he had simply failed to notice the man at all. The offended man refused to be placated, demanding satisfaction on the spot, and drew his sword. Like any gentleman of fashion, Penn was armed. Thanks to the Admiral's training, he was also an expert swordsman; he soon disarmed his opponent, returned his sword to him, and sent him on his way in a less quarrelsome mood. But the episode gave Penn a good deal of food for thought. What kind of a system, he wrote later, could make tipping a hat a matter of "honor," and such "honor" worth a human life? Deeply troubled, in late 1662 or early 1663 he left Paris in search of answers from a famous Protestant theologian, Moïse Amyraut, who was a leading member of the faculty of a seminary at Saumur.

Penn did not enroll at the seminary. For approximately a year, however, he lodged with Amyraut, questioning and listening and clarifying the half-digested ideas he had gleaned from his previous reading. This proved to be one of the most important influences in Penn's development. Amyraut held that the laws of God live in the hearts of men; it followed, therefore, that every man can know right and truth merely by searching his own conscience. This conviction provided the key to what was from that time on Penn's philosophy, political as well as spiritual. Whereas previously he had been drifting, dissatisfied but unclear in his thinking, his ideas now began to coalesce into a solid foundation for his future development.

Early in 1664, however, Amyraut died. With nothing to hold him at Saumur, Penn returned to Paris. There he encountered one of his friends from Oxford, Robert Spencer, who would one day become Earl of Sunderland. Spencer was about to leave for a tour through Provence to Italy and suggested that William join him. The idea was appealing, so the two young Englishmen set out together. Penn found southern France and northern Italy entrancing, but his trip came to an end at Turin when a letter from the Admiral caught up with him: war was expected to break out between England and Holland, and Sir William wanted his son to come home.

Obediently, he parted from Spencer and started back. If war was imminent, it had not yet begun and he traveled by way of Rotterdam. There he met the prominent English political exile, Algernon Sydney, who had opposed the execution of Charles I but was known as a leading advocate of an English republic. Sydney's concept called for a government based on popular consent of the governed, whose basic and traditional individual rights as Englishmen would be maintained by the authorities; upholding these rights was the first obligation of government and the prerequisite for its existence. This was a logical application to the political field of the values which Amyraut had expounded for the spiritual, and exerted an equal influence on Penn's thinking.

When Penn finally reached London in August, 1664, however, the new ideas he had absorbed were beneath the surface. To all intents and purposes he was a typical, foppish young gallant, parading the airs, graces, and elaborate dress newly acquired on his Continental tour. Sir William assumed that his tactic had been successful. As the next stage of the young man's development, he decided to enter him in the Inns of Court for the study of law. In early February of 1665, therefore, William was enrolled at Lincoln's Inn.

The curriculum was far from demanding. In any case, he spent only a short time at his legal studies. The war with the Dutch that had been anticipated for months finally began. Sir William, with the title of Great Captain Commander, was put in actual charge of a thirty-eight ship fleet, although nominally the over-all command was held by James, Duke of York, in his capacity as Lord High Admiral. The opportunity to take part in historic events and, not in-

King Charles II, painting from the studio of John Riley, c. 1680-1685 (courtesy, National Portrait Gallery, London).

significantly, to enjoy a close association with so important a personage as the Duke of York was too valuable to forego. Accordingly, William was withdrawn from Lincoln's Inn to accompany his father as a volunteer aide.

Apparently, William enjoyed life aboard the flagship, and he made an impression on the Duke which provided the foundation for what would become a close personal friendship. In late April, however, before serious operations had begun, he was sent with dispatches to London, where Charles II received him warmly and with flattering queries concerning Sir William's welfare. Whatever the reason may be, William did not rejoin the fleet and by the latter part of May had reentered Lincoln's Inn. Once again, though, his studies were interrupted, this time when an outbreak of plague caused the Inns of Court to close at the beginning of June.

The epidemic, which is known to history as the Great London Plague, lasted through August. The terrible death rate brought a spurt of non-conformist religious activity, with a consequent increase in repressive measures by a government which saw in them the threat of subversion of the established order. Already, Parliament had passed the Conventicle Act, which prohibited any gathering for worship except under the auspices of the Church of England. Now it passed the "Five Mile Act," banning any non-conformist preacher from coming within five miles of any corporation or town and requiring a new oath of allegiance to the Crown and the Church of England.

Whether or not Penn was disturbed by the increasing evidences of repression, there were other matters to command his attention. On June 3, the English fleet had defeated the Dutch in the Battle of Lowestoft. Sir William, for the moment, was again a hero. By September, however, when he returned from sea, criticisms began to be heard because, although the Dutch had been beaten at Lowestoft, the Duke of York had unaccountably failed to exploit the victory with a pursuit that could have been decisive. Sir William defended the Duke, but succeeded only in redirecting the criticisms to himself. It was said that during the battle he had been drunk, or that he had turned coward and hidden behind a coil of rope. Old allegations that he had embezzled funds intended to purchase rations for the crews and that he had been dishonest in sharing prize money yielded from the sale of captured ships were revived.

But by defending the Duke of York, the Admiral rendered another valuable service to the Stuarts. James was already suspect on grounds of his Catholicism, and criticism of his naval operations might extend into broader condemnation that could reach dangerous levels. Taking advantage of the welcome diversion Sir William had provided, the King gave tacit endorsement to the charges against him by failing to grant him rewards comparable to those which went to the other victorious commanders. The Admiral's health, increasingly deteriorating from the gout from which he suffered, provided an excuse to keep him at his duties as a Commissioner and away from command at sea. At the same time, the Stuarts were in his debt to a degree which, by clear implication, they acknowledged privately by their continued personal friendship and publicly by the favors shown to him and, after his death, to his son.

At the moment, Sir William had other troubles. The original owner of Shanagarry filed suit to recover possession. Because the King had confirmed the Penn title to the property, the suit had no chance of succeeding, but it nonetheless had to be dealt with. William had never returned to Lincoln's Inn, so in January, 1666 the Admiral sent him to Ireland to handle the matter of the lawsuit and to collect delinquent rents from the estate's tenants.

The task was straightforward and Penn was soon able to leave Shanagarry and spend some time in Dublin enjoying the active social life suitable to his standing. While he was there, a mutiny broke out among troops stationed at Carrickfergus, just east of the capital. Four companies of loyal soldiers under the Earl of Arran were sent to put down the mutiny, and Penn was one of a number of young gallants who went along as gentlemen volunteers. Evidently, he found this taste of soldiering to his liking. It was at this time that he sat for the only portrait which is agreed to be authentic — a portrait which, ironically in view of what was to happen later, depicts him in armor. He had in fact made such a good impression that the Lord Lieutenant of Ireland, the Duke of Ormonde, wrote to Admiral Penn, suggesting that he resign his captaincy of the company garrisoning Kinsale so that his son could be appointed in his place. Far from being pleased, the Admiral was annoyed and sent a terse letter telling his son not to overreach himself. The Lord Lieutenant had proved tolerant in allowing Sir William to enjoy the perquisites of that captaincy *in absentia*, but could not be counted on to allow young Penn also to function in a similarly absentee capacity; the chances were that he would be required to remain at Kinsale, or at least in Ireland, which would prevent the career at court which his father visualized for him.

William, missing his father's point and still intrigued with mili-

William Penn in Armor, a portrait of the founder of Pennsylvania at age twenty-two, in one of several copies of a now-missing earlier painting.

tary life, next applied for appointment as commissary agent for the Kinsale garrison, but met with no more success. On his father's instructions, he returned to England in time to attend the wedding of his sister, Margaret, to Anthony Lowther, a Yorkshire landowner, on February 15, 1667, but he soon returned to Shanagarry to manage the estate until such time as his father should retire to live in Ireland permanently. It was at this point that something happened which put an end to any military ambitions he may still have been harboring.

Visiting Cork one day, he encountered a Quaker woman of his acquaintance. Mentioning that he had once been enormously impressed by a Quaker preacher named Thomas Loe, he said that he would gladly walk a hundred miles to hear Loe again. The woman replied that there was no need to go any such distance; Loe in fact was in Cork, and would be preaching the following day.

Penn made a point of attending the meeting. Deeply moved by Loe's words, he was to write that "at this time . . . the Lord visited me with a certain sound and testimony of His eternal word." Promptly, he announced that his dearest wish was to become a member of the Society of Friends.

During succeeding weeks he enthusiastically sought out Quaker meetings, absorbing and digesting what he heard and gaining clearer understanding of the Quakers and what they stood for. He also gained a more sharply focused appreciation of the abuses and persecution to which they were subjected. Not yet fully imbued with the Quaker philosophy of non-violence, his initial reaction to the injustices he saw was to fight back.

This was illustrated dramatically on September 3, when a soldier tried to break up a Quaker meeting at Cork which Penn was attending. Penn was outraged and, seizing the man, would have thrown him out of the room if the others present had not dissuaded him. Unmollified, the soldier complained to a magistrate; troops were sent, and they arrested Penn and eighteen others. Mayor Christopher Rye, with the nineteen prisoners arraigned before him, said that as Penn was dressed as a gentleman, wearing a sword, he clearly could not be a Quaker and must have been arrested by mistake, only to have the young man insist firmly that he was indeed a Friend and would not be treated differently from the others. With this, he demanded to know the charge on which they were being held. Told that they had violated the act forbidding more than five Quakers to gather "under pretense of worship," Penn countered that the law had been passed in error, and properly applied only to the "Fifth

Monarchists," but his argument had no effect and all were led off to prison.

From his cell, Penn immediately fired off a letter to the Earl of Orrery, Lord President of Munster, complaining of the mayor's unwarranted action. This quickly brought his release, but it marked the end only of the first of many times that he would go to prison for the sake of the beliefs he had now embraced.

Years of Travail

When word of this arrest reached the Admiral, he ordered his son to come home and explain himself. By the time William arrived at Wanstead, however, his father had reason not only to be angry with his son but worried for himself. The allegations of misbehavior at the Battle of Lowestoft and mishandling of naval funds had been formalized and he was about to face impeachment proceedings. To the Admiral's outraged dismay, William not only refused to abandon his unsuitable new beliefs and associates but announced that he was going on tour as a missionary preacher to spread the Quaker philosophy. In fact, at one such meeting William was arrested, although he was released as soon as he was identified as Admiral Penn's son. All the same, this episode brought on the explosion that had been building up, and William abruptly left home, under orders not to return until he was ready to be sensible. By the spring of 1668, the impeachment had been dropped and Sir William returned to his post in London, but the younger William was actively planning his missionary effort and the breach between father and son remained unhealed.

Penn found that there was much that he could do. With most Quakers being small shopkeepers or rural laborers, he had a social position which gave him an access to court circles which was not available to other members of the Society of Friends. He was prompt to use this asset to act as an advocate for Quakers being held in prison for practicing their beliefs. He also became embroiled in arguments with critics of the Quakers, engaging in exchanges of pamphlets and broadsides and in face-to-face disputes. One of these latter began a series of events which had major consequences.

It came about after a Presbyterian minister named Thomas Vincent made what Penn considered particularly offensive attacks on Quakers and their beliefs. In late October, Penn challenged Vincent to a public debate. Vincent agreed, on condition that the meeting take place at his chapel. When the appointed day arrived, however, Penn and the group of Quakers with him found the building packed with Vincent's followers. Vincent spoke first, holding forth for several hours. Among other objectionable statements that he made was his assertion, completely ignoring the fact that Quakers considered taking oaths for any purpose to be contrary to God's law, that because Penn would not take an oath to abjure the Pope he was actually a Jesuit. Given the temper of the era, that was tantamount to a charge of treason. As soon as Vincent had finished, he and his congregation left without giving William a chance to present his own argument.

The Presbyterian continued his attack in print, with a pamphlet entitled *The Foundations of God Standeth*. Penn replied with a pamphlet of his own, *Sandy Foundations Shaken*. Written in haste, it was ambiguous and could be read as challenging the doctrine of the Trinity and the divinity of Christ, which would make it an attack on the Established Church and therefore on the Crown. Consequently, on December 12 William was imprisoned in the Tower and informed that he would not be released until he repudiated the views he had expressed. At the same time, the Bishop of London arranged for the royal chaplain, Dr. Edward Stillingfleet, to visit the prisoner and reason with him.

Penn found his discussions with Stillingfleet to be stimulating, and the two became friends; but the Quaker's views remained firm and he continued to insist on his right to freedom of conscience. He did, however, publish another pamphlet, *Innocency with Its Open Face: An Apology for Sandy Foundations Shaken,* making it clear that he had never attacked the Church of England and insisting that, on the contrary, he had actually been defending it against Vincent's Presbyterian heresies. The Admiral had also petitioned the Privy Council requesting William's release, and William himself had formally requested release on the grounds that he had been held simply at the behest of the Bishop of London without being granted every Englishman's basic right to a fair trial. In combination, these actions finally brought Penn's discharge from the Tower on July 28, 1669, seven and a half months after having been arrested.

The time he had spent in prison had not been wasted. Perhaps most importantly, Penn had written the first version of what, in the expanded form it took some years later, would be one of his most significant works, *No Cross, No Crown*. In this, he argued for an abandonment of the pomp and ceremony of religious showiness in favor of genuine conviction and virtuous simplicity. Even at this

No Cross, No Crown.

A DISCOURSE

Shewing the
Nature and *Discipline*
Of the HOLY

Cross of Christ,

And That
The *Denyal* of *SELF*, and daily
Bearing of **Christ's Cross**, is the alone
Way to the *Rest* and *Kingdom* of *God*.

To which are added,
The *Living* and *Dying Testimonies* of divers Persons of Fame and Learning, in favour of this *Treatise*.

By *William Penn*.

And Jesus said unto his Disciples; If any Man will come after me, let him Deny himself, and take up his daily CROSS, *and follow me,* Luke 19. 23.
I have fought a Good Fight, I have finished my Course, I have kept the Faith: Henceforth there is laid up for me a CROWN *of Righteousness, which the Lord the Righteous Judge shall give me at that Day; and not me only, but unto all them also, that love his Appearing,* 1 Tim. 4. 7, 8.

The *Second Edition*, Corrected and much Enlarged

London, Printed and Sold by *Benjamin Clark*, Bookseller in *George-Yard* in *Lombard-street*. 1682.

Title page of the book *No Cross, No Crown,* one of William Penn's numerous religious works.

time the pamphlet had considerable impact. Moreover, as a prominent martyr to his beliefs, Penn had gained stature in the eyes of the Society of Friends, who now looked on him as one of their leaders and sought his advice and direction in settling numerous questions. Finally, his difficulties softened the Admiral's attitude, and the two men reconciled their quarrel. At the same time, to reduce the likelihood of new conflicts with the authorities, in September Sir William sent his son to Shanagarry, where once more there were estate problems requiring attention. Before leaving London William hired a Quaker of his acquaintance, Philip Ford, to go with him to serve as steward of the estate.

On Penn's journey from London to Bristol, where he would take ship for Ireland, he visited a succession of Quaker groups. One stop was in Buckinghamshire at the home of long-time friends, Isaac Penington and his step-daughter, Gulielma Maria Springett. According to some accounts, it may have been during this stay that William's proposal of marriage to Gulielma was accepted. If that was in fact the case, theirs was to be an unusually long engagement.

It was late October when Penn finally reached Cork. There, as elsewhere in Ireland, he found that large numbers of Quakers were in prison. Interceding with the local officials, he was able to obtain permission to visit the prisoners and to hold religious meetings for them, but initially he failed to win their release or even to persuade the authorities to promise to treat them more leniently. But he was persistent, and after several weeks of dogged pleading with the ruling figures at Dublin, many of them friends of his father, he secured an order compelling the various mayors to set free the Quakers they were holding.

Turning then to the business for which he had been sent to Ireland, he took care of the estate matters that were critical, after which he left the routine management of Shanagarry to Philip Ford and moved into lodgings at Cork, where he occupied himself writing pamphlets and traveling about to Quaker meetings. During one such absence, the Mayor of Cork ordered his lodgings raided and his books seized. Once again Penn protested to higher authority. The result was that the books were returned and the mayor was reprimanded—but only for having acted in an unseemly way toward a gentleman of Penn's quality.

Elsewhere, more Quakers had been jailed, so Penn renewed his pleas at Dublin. By June of 1670 he was able to obtain an order for their release. It could have been with some satisfaction, therefore, that he left, early in August, for England. Unfortunately, however, events had already given new life to the policy of persecuting nonconformists.

Charles II was secretly plotting with France, a Catholic country, to go to war against Protestant Holland and Sweden. In order to reassure an aggressively Protestant Parliament, he had promoted a renewal of the Conventicle Act. While this was aimed at preventing Catholics from meeting to conspire under the guise of holding religious services, it was being applied equally to all non-conformist sects.

Penn, consulting with other Quaker leaders, decided to provoke a test case which, it was hoped, would establish that Quaker meetings were politically innocent and provide a precedent for their exemption from the Act's restraints. Accordingly, he announced that on August 14, he and William Mead, a Quaker merchant, would hold a religious service. On the appointed day, finding the doors of the meetinghouse blocked by constables, the two men and a group of Quakers gathered in the street. Penn and Mead submitted peaceably to arrest, but a scuffle broke out in the crowd that had collected, so the charge was changed from violation of the Conventicle Act, which would be handled by a summary court, to conspiracy to incite a riot. That was a considerably more serious offense and required a jury trial.

Pending the trial, Penn and Mead were not actually jailed but were allowed to stay at a tavern near Newgate prison. On September 3, the case came up before Sir Samuel Starling, the Lord Mayor of London. As the two prisoners entered the courtroom, the bailiff snatched their hats off their heads, but Sir Samuel ordered the man to replace them; then, contending that the two Quakers were in contempt of court for failing to uncover before him, he imposed a fine. Penn and Mead refused to pay, arguing that they had in fact been bareheaded before the judge until he himself ordered his own official to replace their hats. Angrily, Sir Samuel rejected this argument, and the fine stood.

The trial continued in the same vein. Starling openly showed his prejudice by making slighting remarks about Sir William Penn "who starved the sailors." He allowed only prosecution witnesses to be called, and would not allow them to be cross examined by Penn, who was functioning as his own and Mead's defense counsel. One travesty followed another, so blatantly that the jury became completely alienated and delivered a verdict that Mead was innocent and that Penn was guilty only of speaking in the street. Sir Samuel berated the jurors and sent them back to reconsider, but they returned the same verdict. Refusing to accept this finding, Starling again abused them, and said that they would be held without food or drink until they came back with a finding of guilty.

This altered the whole situation. In effect, the jury system itself was now at stake. Led by their foreman, Edward Bushell, the jurors clearly recognized the issue and, although the judge held to his threat, keeping them isolated for two days without meals or even access to sanitary facilities, they still would not budge. When finally recalled, the jury announced that it had indeed changed its verdict—*now* it found that Penn as well as Mead was innocent of all charges. Sir Samuel, furious, fined each juror for contempt and, since neither they nor the two Quakers would pay any of the fines that had been imposed, sent all of them to jail in Newgate—the prison for common criminals.

Penn's father, now on his deathbed, urged his son to pay the fine, but William stood on principle and remained in prison until the Admiral himself paid for both William and Mead, and they were freed. (Eight of the twelve jurors also gave in, but Bushell and three others would not, remaining in jail until, after two months, they were released on bail. Some four years later, when their appeal was finally considered, the Lord Chief Justice upheld them in a landmark decision which confirmed a jury's freedom from coercion from the bench.)

Penn was released in time for a reconciliation with his father, who died within a week. Shortly after the Admiral's funeral, William began working with Mead in writing a broadside exposing and challenging Sir Samuel Starling's actions on the bench. This provoked an answering pamphlet from Starling, who gratuitously included an attack on Sir William's naval record. In turn, that brought a pamphlet from Penn, *Truth Rescued from Impostors,* which consisted of a defense of his father against the various slanders and libels that had been circulated.

This done, he plunged again into efforts to defend Quaker rights and beliefs, resuming his activities as a traveling preacher. He won converts, but was soon arrested and tried again. On a technicality, he was found innocent of preaching in violation of the Five Mile Act, but was sentenced to six months in jail for refusing to swear an oath that taking up arms against the King was unlawful. Once more he was sent to Newgate.

Again, he used the time to write, producing a number of treatises, perhaps the most important being *The Great Case of Liberty of Conscience,* in which he combined and synthesized his convictions regarding religious freedom and political rights. When his sentence was completed in August, 1671, he left for a two-month visit with progressive religious groups in the Netherlands and Germany, exchanging ideas and seeking converts.

On Penn's return to England in the fall of 1671, he found himself for the time being called upon to substitute for George Fox, the organizational and administrative leader of the Society of Friends, who had left for an extended visit to America shortly after Penn's release from Newgate. This brought new and demanding responsibilities. However, these did not interfere completely with his personal life, for on April 4, 1672, he and Gulielma Maria Springett finally were married, settling at Rickmansworth, in Hertfordshire. As Sir William's eldest son, Penn had inherited substantial property, and Gulielma was even wealthier. They were able to live in comfort, without financial worries, and Penn was left with full leisure to devote all his activities to the affairs of the Society of Friends. Moreover, he was soon able to carry these out without having to fear official reprisals. Charles II, to promote national unity for his war against the Dutch, sought to end dissension at home by issuing a Declaration of Indulgence permitting non-conformists to worship freely. The return of George Fox in July, 1673 also relieved Penn of his administrative responsibilities, so that he was able to concentrate more exclusively on his preaching and his writing, which now was devoted chiefly to eradicating the general misunderstandings of Quaker beliefs which prompted most of the popular criticism and persecution.

However, conditions did not long remain favorable. Within a short time, Parliament not only nullified the Declaration of Indulgence but imposed the Test Act, which required every public official to be a communicant of the Church of England and to swear allegiance to the King. In itself, this posed no threat to Quakers, who did not seek public office. The problem was that their beliefs prohibited them from swearing oaths of any type. Since they were generally viewed with suspicion, they were often arrested on trivial charges which would not stand up under any sort of judicial process, but before they were released they would be directed to demonstrate their loyalty by swearing allegiance to the Crown. This, of course, they refused to do. In complete disregard of the reasons for this stand, the authorities would insist that the Quakers' refusal to swear the oath demanded was evidence of disloyalty and doubtless indicated a secret loyalty to Protestant England's archenemy, the Pope. Once again, the prisons began to fill with Quakers, and in mid-December George Fox himself was arrested.

The charge was preposterous. Penn flung himself vigorously into an effort to secure Fox's release. Aside from intensive study of the legal factors involved, he made approaches to the various contacts he had at court, in particular to his father's friend, the Duke of York.

As a Catholic, the Duke had a considerable fellow-feeling for non-conformists, and both he and Charles II were as tolerant of religion as Parliament would permit. Beyond that, he and Penn quickly developed a mutual liking and respect which grew into a warm and lasting friendship. All the same, it would not be until January of 1675 that Penn and his supporters would be able to win freedom for Fox.

Throughout this period, Penn had suffered a series of personal tragedies. His only brother, Richard, had died. William and Gulielma had become the parents of a daughter and then of twins, a boy and a girl, all of whom died in infancy. The one bright spot was that, despite his prominence and his activities, he himself was not made subject to the official harassment and persecution directed against Quakers in general.

It was during these months that he became actively interested in the idea of a Quaker settlement in America. His direct involvement began in the fall of 1674, when he was asked to arbitrate a dispute between two Quakers, John Fenwick and Edward Byllinge (or Billinge). Fenwick claimed that he had given Byllinge a loan of a thousand pounds with which to buy the southern part of New Jersey, known as "West Jersey," from its proprietor, John, Lord Berkeley. Because Byllinge was deeply in debt and his creditors could be expected to argue that any funds coming into his hands should go to settle his accounts with them, the actual purchase had been made by Fenwick, in trust for Byllinge. Subsequently, however, Byllinge claimed that the thousand pounds had been his, and that Fenwick was entitled only to a fee for his services as purchasing agent.

Penn's ruling was that the money was indeed Byllinge's, but that Fenwick should be allowed to buy one-tenth of West Jersey for a hundred pounds, the remainder of the territory going to Byllinge. To satisfy his creditors, Byllinge immediately transferred administrative control of his share to a three-man board of trustees, of whom Penn was one, and they began selling tracts of land, using part of the sums obtained to pay off Byllinge's debts.

The question of governmental authority in the prospective colony was ambiguous, however (it would not be formally settled until late

1683), so Penn and his associates moved very methodically to clarify the relations that would prevail between the Crown, the proprietors and the Quaker colonists they hoped to attract. Fenwick, by contrast, immediately began selling land and by June of 1675 had led a group of 120 settlers to America. It was not until 1677 that the trustees of the larger portion of West Jersey launched their own colonizing effort, with 230 settlers. Despite the different approaches, the settlements took root and grew. The whole undertaking, moreover, gave Penn experience that was to prove valuable in the future. In particular, working with his colleagues, he was able to incorporate many of his political ideas into a document (much of it probably written by Byllinge) entitled "Concessions and Agreements" which foreshadowed the structure he would later develop for Pennsylvania and, in many significant respects, the United States Constitution. It provided complete freedom of religion, vested the power of government in the people themselves, affirmed the basic English rights and freedoms, and in sum represented in one document the most enlightened and liberal governmental structure then in existence.

While Penn was still involved in arbitrating the Fenwick-Byllinge dispute his son, Springett, was born. Not long afterward, he moved his family from Rickmansworth — the location, he thought, was unhealthy, and he blamed it for the deaths of his first three children — to Worminghurst, in Sussex. In 1677 he left, this time with George Fox and others, on another missionary tour of the Low Countries and Germany. Again, most of the people he encountered received him hospitably and listened courteously, although only a comparative few joined the Society of Friends, and some openly disputed the message he tried to spread. At the same time, he established contacts which were to result directly in an influx of Palatine Germans into Pennsylvania a few years later.

Penn was out of England from July until October. While he was gone, there was another upsurge in harassment of the non-conformist sects. For several months after his return, therefore, his time was taken up in traveling about the country gathering details of the persecutions, meeting with other leading Quakers to plan the courses of action to be followed in defending specific cases, and helping to resolve doctrinal and organizational disputes which had arisen within the Society of Friends. On March 6, 1678, while he was busied in this fashion, his daughter Letitia was born.

That same month, in a major effort to achieve some easing of the treatment of non-conformists, Penn appeared before a committee of Parliament, pleading for an amendment to the Test Act which would permit Quakers to affirm their loyalty to the King rather than having to swear an oath. In the process, he repeated his conviction that every person, even a Catholic, should be free to worship as his conscience dictated. He convinced the House of Commons, but Parliament was prorogued before the House of Lords had a chance to act on the amendment.

Penn's success with Parliament, on the other hand, made him a target of strong criticism from the public. Even many of his fellow Quakers were critical of his contention that Catholics should have freedom of worship, a number adding their voices to the revived clamor that Penn was himself a secret Catholic. In addition to citing his refusal to swear allegiance to the King as evidence of loyalty to the Pope, it was said that he would not take off his hat lest he be revealed as a tonsured priest, and that his stay at the Protestant seminary at Saumur had actually been an enrollment at the Jesuit seminary at St. Omer. His problems were compounded when his former neighbor at Rickmansworth, Titus Oates, proclaimed that a Catholic plot existed to assassinate Charles II and replace him with his avowedly Catholic brother and Penn's friend, James, Duke of York.

There was no truth to Oates's allegations, but Penn was the object of unfriendly official surveillance for a protracted period. His situation was not improved when, in 1679, he supported his friend, Algernon Sydney, in an unsuccessful bid for election to Parliament. How Penn could have been pro-Catholic and at the same time support Sydney, a Puritan and a man who had advocated republican government, is difficult to comprehend, but the incompatibility of the positions attributed to Penn did not deter his critics.

The personal attacks and the general decline of morality in England depressed Penn severely. He was further disillusioned at Sydney's defeat at the polls, for one of his most cherished convictions was that, given freedom of choice, ordinary men would always choose the right. For all his belief in religious tolerance, Penn was unable then or later to comprehend that individual perceptions of right and wrong often differ, and he could not understand how the voters could have failed to elect the man who, to Penn's mind, was so indisputably the proper candidate.

At least some of the matters in which Penn was involved, however, were going well. In his personal life, his son William, Jr. was born in March, 1680. On another level, the West Jersey colony was prospering in a generally satisfactory way. But increasingly, Penn was becoming seriously interested in the idea of establishing a completely new colony which, while it would be open to people of all beliefs, would be predominantly a refuge for Quakers.

As it happened, at one stage during his service under the Stuarts Sir William had used substantial sums from his own pocket to pay for rations for the crews of his ships. He had never been reimbursed, and by this time the amount, with interest, had grown to sixteen thousand pounds. This sum in theory was owed to Sir William's estate; but Charles II, faced with large numbers of similar obligations, had simply declared a moratorium on all such debts. Legally, therefore, Penn had no basis for any claim against the Crown.

On the other hand, the debt might provide an ostensible justification for requesting a grant of land in America. Stronger if unacknowledged reasons were that such a concession might quiet the Protestant criticism that Charles and James were leaning too much in favor of the Catholics, and it certainly would remove from England numbers of Quakers who, if they caused no actual trouble, were a perennial source of dissension.

It was on June 1, 1680 that Penn formally petitioned the Crown for a grant of the territory extending for five degrees of longitude west of the Delaware River between New York on the north and Maryland on the south. His old friend, Robert Spencer, now Earl of Sunderland and a Secretary of State, supported the petition. Negotiations continued through October, with approval being obtained successively from the various agencies concerned. Considering the administrative intricacies, remarkably rapid progress was made—although the process was undeniably speeded by Penn's disbursement to various officials of "gratuities" which totaled, he wrote, almost sixteen hundred pounds. Penn himself drafted the bulk of the patent, with modifications inserted by the Lord Chief Justice and the Attorney General to safeguard Crown interests. A further change was imposed by the King himself: Charles II wanted to commemorate the Admiral and insisted that the new Province be named Pennsylvania. Penn feared that such a name would appear to be an attempt at his own self-glorification and offered a gratuity of twenty guineas to Sir Leoline Jenkins, the Secretary of State preparing the final version of the patent, to alter the name to either "Sylvania" or "New Wales," but Sir Leoline was unwilling to disregard the King's instructions, and refused. (In an effort to fend off the criticism he feared, Penn then circulated the ingenuous explanation that the name was derived from the Welsh word for hill—"Penn"—so that the new Province was to be known by a composite

The first page of the charter by which Charles II granted proprietorship of Pennsylvania to William Penn.

word describing the terrain.) On March 4 (March 14, New Style), 1681, Charles II affixed his signature and seal on the document, known since as the Charter. Thereby William Penn, in return only for an annual "peppercorn rent" of two beaver skins and one-fifth of any gold or silver that might be discovered, became the sole proprietor of the largest territory ever owned outright by any British subject in history.

The New Colony

In its delineation of the territory concerned, the Charter which Charles II granted to William Penn was at best confusing. The boundary between Pennsylvania and Maryland, in particular, was ambiguously defined. Maryland's northern limit had been fixed as a specified number of miles north of a point believed (incorrectly) to be at the 38th parallel of latitude to what was believed (also incorrectly) to be the 40th parallel. Pennsylvania's southeastern boundary was to be established by a circle, drawn at a radius of twelve miles from the town of New Castle, extending from the Delaware River to the west and south until it reached the east-west line running through New Castle which, the Charter stated, was the 40th parallel. In actual fact, the 40th degree of latitude lies many miles to the north—indeed, it is well above what were for decades the northern limits of Philadelphia. This lack of precision was to produce a series of disputes which would not be settled for at least seventy years.

As delineated, the territory suffered the major disadvantage that it had no outlet to the open sea. The western bank of the Delaware River from the point specified above New Castle southward was part of territory later known as "the three lower counties" which was claimed both by Lord Baltimore, the Proprietor of Maryland, and the Duke of York. In order to obtain the economically vital access to the sea, Penn began negotiations aimed at persuading the Duke of York to grant this area to him.

Within Pennsylvania itself, Penn was granted sweeping authority. He had full powers to create and fill offices, except that any nominee for Deputy Governor had to be approved by the Crown. In his own absence from England, he was to maintain an agent for the colony in or near London. He could make such laws as he chose, with the consent of the freemen of the Province, provided that no law was contrary to the laws of England. The one qualification was that Pennsylvania was unique among the British colonies in America in that within five years after enactment of a law, it must be submitted to London for approval. He could establish counties, towns and seaports. Other than by royal edict or Act of Parliament, no taxes could be imposed without his consent and that of the Province's freemen. He was also granted the unwanted authority to raise a militia, but he was not entitled to wage war on his own initiative—a restriction which certainly did not disturb him. Neither would he have been troubled by the requirement to permit the Church of England to establish a clergyman in Pennsylvania for any twenty inhabitants so requesting. He intended to live at peace with everyone, and he was determined to maintain complete freedom of worship. All trade and commerce were to be with Britain, of course, but this requirement existed for all colonies in America.

Once the Charter was signed, Penn lost no time in launching his project. On April 10 he appointed a Deputy Governor, his cousin William Markham, who promptly left for Pennsylvania to institute a preliminary government, to select locations for a capital city and for the residence Penn would occupy as soon as he himself could emigrate, and to establish friendly relations with the Indians, the neighboring colonies, and the thousand or so settlers (primarily Dutch and Swedish) already in the area. Meanwhile, Penn plunged into promotion of sales of land in the Province.

To advertise the opportunity he offered, he published two treatises, *A Brief Account of the Province of Pennsylvania* and the considerably more comprehensive pamphlet, *Some Account of the Province of Pennsylvania*. The latter contained so much new information (not all of it accurate) on climate, soil, vegetation, natives, wildlife and geography that, although Penn himself had not yet laid eyes on the territory he described so glowingly, it brought his election as a Fellow of the Royal Society for his contributions to scientific knowledge.

Penn did not restrict his promotional efforts to Great Britain. Taking advantage of the acquaintances he had made during his trips to the Continent, he sent word to his correspondents in Germany, Holland and France. He was particularly hopeful of being able to attract Frenchmen who could establish industries for the production of silk and wine.

He offered one hundred 5,000-acre tracts for one hundred pounds each, along with smaller packets of land, but he also imposed an annual quitrent of one shilling for each hundred acres, to fall due after 1684. In addition, he offered transportation at the rate of fifty shillings for children under ten, five pounds for servants, and six pounds for other adults. His prices were substantially higher than those charged in 1675 for land in West Jersey: John Fenwick had sold a thousand acres for a mere five pounds (only one-fourth of Penn's price per acre) and had provided passage at fifty shillings for children up to age twelve and at only five pounds for others. Penn's sales of large tracts, in fact, were slow, and in the course of a year less than half of the hundred that he had hoped to dispose of had been taken up.

Despite the higher prices, however, smaller tracts (averaging 750 acres) sold rapidly. Comparatively few of the purchasers were farmers; most, Penn was pleased to note, were artisans and craftsmen. As early as July, the colony was showing signs of growth as successive shiploads of settlers began to leave England. Penn was also glad to learn that some Germans were joining the English, Irish, Welsh and Scottish emigrants, although he was disappointed that few of the French he had hoped to attract were showing interest.

The purchasers who had not yet departed met with Penn and drew up provisional terms of agreement on legal, commercial and property relationships to apply to Penn, the settlers and the Indians. This agreement also specified that in the city which was to be laid out, each of the "First Purchasers"—that is, those who bought land between 1681 and 1685—would receive a bonus grant of ten acres for every five hundred acres he had bought. It was further provided that the agreement would be tentative until all the European inhabitants already in Pennsylvania had been given the opportunity to approve, modify or reject it.

The city which Penn visualized was to be the fulfillment of a concept to which he had devoted particular attention. It would avoid the congestion of the crowded cities of Europe with their narrow, twisting streets, their lack of fresh air and vegetation, and their susceptibility to epidemics, crime and spreading conflagrations. The space from the waterfront for a quarter of a mile inland was to be kept free of buildings. There would be two broad, straight, tree-lined avenues, one running north and south and the other east and west, with a park at their intersection. Paralleling these in a regular grid would be streets (also lined with trees) which, while narrower than the avenues, would still be much wider than was normal in Europe. Each quarter of the city would have its own park. Houses were to be sited in a straight line along the streets, but each was to be located in the center of its lot so as to leave space on either side "for gardens or orchards, or fields, that it may be a green country town, which will never be burned, and always be wholesome." In the event, the population of the city would grow too rapidly to permit leaving open the amount of space Penn had intended, but important elements of his concept were preserved. And although Penn cannot be said to have originated the idea of a regular grid arrangement of streets, he certainly revived it after centuries of disuse, thereby setting an example which left a permanent imprint in its influence on cities that have since come into being.

The provisional terms of agreement adopted at this time were the forerunner of the more detailed constitution, the "First Frame of Government," which was the fruit of careful thinking and wide consultation by Penn during the next several months. The structure it established comprised the Governor—that is, the Proprietor or his appointed Deputy Governor—a General Assembly (initially with two hundred members), and a seventy-two-man Council. The Proprietor of course held his office by heredity, but the Assembly and the Council were to be elected by the freemen of the Province. The Governor, with three votes, presided over the Council and in concert with it was charged with all executive powers, together with the authority to convene or dissolve the Assembly and to initiate legislation. The powers of the General Assembly were limited to approving or rejecting, without the right to debate or amend, the legislation proposed by the Governor and Council. Although some more liberal political thinkers, Algernon Sydney among them, criticized the weakness of the Assembly and others protested the failure to ban slavery or the slave trade, the facts remained that the far more powerful Council was also a popularly elected body and that no one man, including the Proprietor, could impose his will on the whole.

Freedom of elections was expressly insured. The right to vote was extended to virtually all free inhabitants, regardless of whether they were landholders or whether they were British subjects. No taxes could be imposed except by law, courts were to be open, and jury trial—with the juries being explicitly free to interpret laws and return verdicts without challenge—was guaranteed, as was bail in all but capital cases. Remembering the horrors he had observed in Newgate, Penn went into considerable detail concerning treatment of prisoners: fees for wardens, food, heat and lodging were not to be charged, and emphasis was to be placed on rehabilitation rather than on punishment. Another progressive social reform was that all children over twelve were to be taught a trade or skill. A moralistic note was struck by the prohibition of gambling, stage plays, drunkenness, profanity, scandal-mongering and lying, and by the provision that First Days were to be devoted to rest and religious observances. Freedom of worship was guaranteed, but as the law was eventually applied, no one could vote or hold office unless he professed his belief in Jesus Christ as the Son of God and the Savior of the World.

Viewed as either a political or a social document, this constitution reflects concepts that, for their time, were remarkably advanced. In many respects the principles it embodies represent the first application of rights and values which, while largely taken for granted today, are looked on as fundamental to American liberty.

While Penn was working diligently to prepare to see his new colony for himself, he suffered a heavy personal blow when, late in the winter of 1682, his mother died. But the demands of his project were so pressing that he could not indulge himself in lengthy mourning. Aside from refining the draft of the First Frame of Government, he had to take every action he could to establish a firm foundation for the Province. In particular, there was the question of the southeastern boundary and access to the sea. Not until August was his request for a grant of the land on the west bank of the Delaware River — the "three lower counties" — finally processed and approved by the Duke of York. Although the Duke's title to the territory had not yet been confirmed and the ownership remained ambiguous, this action did improve the situation in Penn's eyes.

It was at this time, also, that he completed his most important theological treatise, the new version of *No Cross, No Crown*. It was not merely a revision, but a vastly more completely developed and penetrating exposition of his interpretation of Quaker doctrine, reflecting the maturity brought by almost a decade and a half of thought and experience. The cross of which he spoke was conformity with the will of God; the crown was the achievement of the soul's salvation. He was not preaching a doctrine of withdrawal from the world, much less a doctrine of masochism or even of foregoing comfort and ease. He did, however, advocate simplicity, holding that self-denial of luxury and indulgence was essential to complying with God's will. Man was not inherently evil; on the contrary, as God's handiwork, he was inherently good. For that reason, such worldly distinctions as titles and status, and the ceremony which collected around them, setting some people apart from their fellows, were to be avoided. All men were deserving of equal respect and equal consideration.

This work completed, he was ready to depart with his family for America. Almost at the last minute, however, his wife's health made it necessary for her to remain behind, and the children stayed with her. But in late August, with about a hundred prospective settlers, Penn himself sailed from Deal on the bark *Welcome*.

The voyage was marked by hardship even beyond what was normal for those times, for while the *Welcome* was en route smallpox broke out. Having survived a bout with the disease as a small child, Penn was immune, and was consequently able to devote himself to the task of helping to nurse the sick. For approximately a third of the passengers, however, the illness proved fatal, so it was a sorely depleted group which, after some two months at sea, arrived about sunset on October 27 at New Castle. There, on October 28, Penn ceremonially took possession of the town and its surrounding territory. Reembarking, he sailed up the Delaware to the village of Upland and went ashore to set foot at last on land in Pennsylvania proper.

After announcing that he was changing the name of the town to Chester, he created three new counties—Philadelphia, Chester and

The Landing of William Penn, a fanciful painting by Thomas Birch (courtesy, Museum of Fine Arts, Boston).

Bucks—and sent out writs to those areas and to the three existing "lower" counties (New Castle, Kent and Sussex), summoning the freeholders to a meeting at Chester on December 4. In the meantime, he hoped to meet with Lord Baltimore to inform him of the Duke of York's grant, but Baltimore requested a delay. Penn used the time to make a quick circuit, calling on the Governor of New York, visiting Quaker meetings on Long Island, then proceeding by way of West Jersey to Philadelphia and the site of what was to be his own estate at Pennsbury. He may also have met with a group of Indians, including the Delaware chief Tamamend (whose name was corrupted by tradition to "Tammany"), at Shackamaxon, a few miles north of the planned location of Philadelphia.

At Chester on December 4, Penn found that only about half of the freeholders had chosen to answer his summons. These, however, rapidly approved the draft constitution, with some modifications. All residents were automatically granted citizenship, the minimum voting age was fixed at twenty-one, taxes would be enacted for only one year at a time, and the three lower counties were united with Pennsylvania. The complete document, known as the Great Law, was adopted on December 7. Four days later, Penn left Chester for his postponed visit with Lord Baltimore. So far as reaching any settlement of the disputed boundary was concerned, the meeting was a failure, but the two Proprietors did agree to meet again at a later date.

The first session of the newly established popular government took place on March 12, 1683, at Philadelphia. Already, however, Penn had introduced changes: deciding that the numbers specified in the First Frame of Government were unwieldy, he had asked each county to elect only six members to the Assembly and three to the Council. Almost at once he began to find that his assumption that good men would always have identical views of what was right was unfounded. He had taken it for granted that Quakers would predominate, but as it turned out, they comprised little more than half the membership. Next, the Assembly asked for the right to initiate legislation and to debate and amend bills proposed by the Council. The Council, moreover, objected to the Governor having three votes. Dispute not only became heated but, as was common in that era, opposing groups and individuals (including Penn himself) attacked each other's motives and integrity in terms that were personal, intemperate and abusive. The upshot was general recognition that the original Frame of Government ought to be altered.

The Second Frame of Government, adopted on April 2, 1683,

fell somewhat short of meeting the more extreme demands. Penn refused to concur in any extensive enlargement of the powers of the Assembly, although with the prior permission of the Council the Assembly was now permitted to initiate and debate bills. Pending increases justified by future population growth, the Assembly was to have thirty-six members and the Council eighteen. In the Council, the Governor would have only one vote. Also, he would have to obtain the Council's advice and consent for any public act he might undertake, although throughout Penn's lifetime he was to be entitled to appoint judges and other officials (from lists provided by the Council), with the appointing authority reverting to the Council after his death. While the matter was not explicitly addressed, he assumed that he retained the right to veto Council actions, and he did win the concession that he was no longer responsible for underwriting the costs of government. (This proved unpopular, as it required a poll tax and involved the further authority for justices to impose taxes to meet government expenses. Adding to dissatisfaction was the fact that many of the settlers had assumed that the quitrents had been intended for this purpose, whereas Penn had visualized the quitrents as serving the dual purposes of symbolizing his feudal Proprietorship and providing a source of personal income.)

In brief, the Second Frame of Government, for all its merits, laid the foundations of two of the disputes—over the powers of the Assembly and the financial obligations of the colony to the Proprietor—which for years to come would complicate the relations between Penn and the people of Pennsylvania.

When the Assembly and Council adjourned, Penn resumed his effort to reach an agreement over the southeastern boundary. In the interest of harmony, he offered to buy the territory in dispute, provided Lord Baltimore would accept at once; otherwise, Penn would lay the issue before the King. Lord Baltimore inferred that this was a tacit acknowledgement of the justice of his own claim; but being aware of Penn's connections at court, he was not sure how Charles II might rule. To gain time, he claimed that he was ill and could not address himself to the question until he had recovered.

If the unsettled boundary was troubling, much remained to occupy Penn's attention during the year that followed. Pennsylvania's population was mushrooming, with shiploads of new settlers arriving at the rate of one a week. Along with large numbers of Irish, Welsh, and Scotch-Irish, Germans led by Francis Daniel Pastorius, followed by other Germans from Krefeld, were soon settling in what was to become Germantown. Early in the summer, after arranging for construction of his seat at Pennsbury to start, Penn began extensive travels to explore some of the farther reaches of his domain.

As he passed through the areas of various Indian bands (he called them "nations," each consisting of "perhaps two hundred people"), he met ceremonially in council with their "kings." He made numerous land purchases and repeatedly expounded the policy he was determined to follow toward the Indians.

That policy, which made Pennsylvania's relations with the Indians unique among the colonies, was not new in being based on purchase of the land to be settled. In a number of other respects, however, it was distinctive. Penn had a long-standing interest in and respect for the Indians, whom he viewed as simple children of nature unspoiled by the vices of civilization. This interest led him to develop understanding of their cultural values, permitting him to avoid the ignorance and misunderstanding which, more than viciousness, had led to clashes in other parts of British America. He insisted that the Indians be fairly treated, and did all he could to prevent exploitation of their naiveté and their susceptibility to liquor. At the same time, he would not be imposed upon, and held them firmly to agreements they had made. The result was to be an unparalleled record of some seventy years of almost completely unbroken peaceful association.

Despite the rapid progress that was being made throughout the colony, some old problems got worse and new ones arose.

Because of the outlay of cash that had been required, Penn began to worry about money matters. He complained that besides the gratuities he had paid to process his patent, he had been put during the first year alone to an expense of at least five thousand pounds without obtaining any financial return. This led him to ask the Assembly to authorize the early payment of the quitrents. As the sales agreements had stipulated that these would not be due until 1684, the Assembly refused. The settlers had little cash in any case, and because they thought of Penn as one of the richest men in England they began to consider him grasping and hypocritical. When as a substitute for early payment of the quitrents he asked for a tax on alcoholic beverages, the Assembly approved the tax but promptly suspended its collection "to encourage trade."

On the south, Lord Baltimore not only had not given up his claims but was growing truculent. For a time, a body of Maryland militia actually moved into territory claimed by Penn, attempted to collect Maryland taxes, and began building a fort. Without a militia of its own and being committed as a matter of principle to a

William Penn maintained peaceful relations in his dealings with the Native Americans. This concord is celebrated in *Penn's Treaty with the Indians*, c. 1830 by Edward Hicks. A gift of Meyer P. and Vivian Potamkin to The State Museum of Pennsylvania.

policy of non-violence, Pennsylvania was unable to take any action against the intruders.

Finally, not all of the new settlers were as high minded as Penn had expected. The large profits to be made from dealing directly with non-British merchants were an invitation to violate the Navigation Acts, and it was not long before royal officials caught a French ship trading illegally. Along the Delaware, in fact, these officials reported that smuggling and piracy were widespread. These developments could be expected to raise questions in London concerning the effectiveness with which Penn was exercising control of his colony.

This was particularly serious. Some factions in London, seeking to consolidate Crown authority, were actively interested in eliminating all of the colonial proprietorships. Combined with the questions Lord Baltimore was raising concerning title to the three lower counties, there was a real possibility, Penn feared, that retention of his charter might be jeopardized. It was little comfort that, if charters were to be canceled, Lord Baltimore was at least as vulnerable. Reluctantly, therefore, Penn decided that in order to protect his interests he would have to return to England.

The Lengthy Absence

On August 12, 1684, Penn sailed from Philadelphia on the ketch *Endeavour,* reaching home on October 6. To his dismay, he found that the documents that were vital for him to support his claim to the three lower counties had somehow been left in Pennsylvania. He sent an urgent demand for them to be forwarded to him as rapidly as possible, but there was little hope that they could arrive in time. To his incredibly good fortune, the Lords Commissioners of the Board of Trade and Plantations deferred the case, and then Lord Baltimore (who also had returned to England) requested a further delay, so that Penn was armed with the papers he required well before the hearing could finally take place.

In the meantime, he was once more confronted with the reality of religious intolerance. Moving about to Quaker meetings to spread the word of developments in Pennsylvania, he was twice indicted for preaching in violation of the law, and fined for participating in illegal assemblies. Some thirteen hundred Quakers, he learned, were in prison as non-conformists. Charles II was dying; but the Duke of York, who would succeed him, promised to release them as soon as his coronation had taken place.

The new King's position after Charles's death on February 6,

1685 was delicate. Openly Catholic, he was suspect in the eyes of Parliament and people. Any leniency he might show toward nonconformists would be taken as the first opening of the door to Catholicism. Compelled to avoid antagonizing such shaky support as he had, he not only delayed fulfilling his promise to release the Quakers but even went so far as to allow the drafting of writs of quo warranto against all proprietary colonies, the first step toward revoking their charters. Nevertheless, Penn insisted to the suspicious Quakers that James II should be trusted.

Within less than five months after his accession, the King faced a further challenge when Charles's illegitimate son, the Duke of Monmouth, raised a rebellion aimed at putting himself on the throne. Penn promptly sent instructions to America, directing Pennsylvanians not to criticize James or express sympathy with Monmouth. With this, to provide some safeguard against charges of inept administration that might be made, he ordered strict observance of the Navigation Acts. Many of Penn's followers in England and America became convinced that in his gullibility he was playing into the hands of the King who, as soon as his position was consolidated, would impose repressive measures on all Protestants.

In the event, Monmouth's rebellion was rapidly suppressed. The preoccupation with this crisis and with punishing the participants had the advantage of causing the movement against the proprietary colonies to be abandoned. But because some of those involved in the uprising were acquaintances of Penn, he himself was for a time under suspicion. Shopworn accusations that Quakers were secret Catholics were revived. In Penn's particular case, his known friendship with James was irrationally cited as "proof" that he was a Catholic, hence disloyal to the throne—even though it was Catholic James who occupied that throne.

Fortunately, the feeling against Quakers in general and Penn in particular had no official basis. Indeed, when in November the Lords Commissioners of the Board of Trade and Plantations finally took the dispute between Penn and Lord Baltimore under consideration, they denied Lord Baltimore's claim. Moreover, in March, 1686, the Quakers in prison for refusing to swear oaths were freed. With regard to Penn specifically, the King issued a warrant that, in recognition of Admiral Penn's services and of William's loyalty and affection, all proceedings against him were to be dropped and he, his family, and his servants were to be exempt from prosecution on religious grounds.

Although these matters were going well, Penn was beset with

King James II, painted c. 1690 by an unknown artist (courtesy, National Portrait Gallery, London).

other worries. His new daughter, born in November, 1685, was not healthy. He was also troubled with money problems: compelled to keep up a residence in London, so that he could protect his interests, and at the same time to support his family home at Worminghurst, he had to meet the expense of maintaining two households; taking on more and more of the administration of the Society of Friends as George Fox declined in health entailed considerable outlay; despite the rulings of the Pennsylvania Assembly, he was still having to underwrite the complete costs of the government of his colony. All this notwithstanding the facts that continuing uprisings in Ireland disrupted the collection of rents from Shanagarry, sales of land in Pennsylvania were declining, and the quitrents due on the land that had been sold were not being collected. Some of his business ventures, also, had been disappointing—he had been outraged at the fee charged by his agent in Pennsylvania for selling a ship's cargo whose transportation Penn had financed, for after the expenses had been deducted the profit remaining had been much smaller than he had expected.

To make matters worse, Philip Ford, who for years had been functioning as Penn's business manager, asked for payment of his wages (several years in arrears), of money he had advanced to Penn from his own pocket, and of interest on both. The sum involved was a substantial 4,293 pounds. For all his other virtues, Penn was a poor manager, and was careless about finances. Having been wealthy all his life, he could not comprehend how anyone could actually have a truly dire need for funds, with the result that even while acknowledging his debts he was prone to feel resentful and mistreated when his creditors tried to collect what was due them. In this case, he persuaded Ford to accept a two-year delay in payment. Other demands he met by selling some of his wife's landholdings and mortgaging others.

By this time, James II was feeling that his position on the throne was sufficiently secure for him to begin working for a relaxation of some of the more severe strictures against non-conformists. Recognizing that Parliament on its own initiative would never agree to repeal of these laws, he was thinking in terms of abolishing at least the Test Act simply by royal decree.

Enlightened though the objective of such action might be, however, in principle it would be dictatorial, for in issuing such a decree the King would be unilaterally overriding the will of the electorate as expressed through its chosen representatives. As a preliminary precaution, therefore, he felt it wise to obtain the views and support of his son-in-law, Prince William of Orange, who was the leading Protestant monarch on the European continent.

To this end, in June, 1686 the King asked Penn to travel to Holland and approach Prince William on the proposal. Despite the conflict this posed between Penn's convictions concerning religious freedom and his ideas on popular government, he readily agreed. He found Prince William receptive to the principle of toleration but opposed to the prospect of establishing it in defiance of Parliament; the Prince would support such action by James II only if the decrees were ratified by Parliament and if his wife, Mary, whose right to succeed James would be jeopardized, were compensated with an annual allowance of forty-eight thousand pounds. Penn could only forward William's offer to the King, and since the parliamentary ratification which the Prince had stipulated was an impossibility, the matter was dropped. It appears, however, that Mary blamed the loss of the proposed forty-eight-thousand-pound pension on Penn, and it has been suggested that the dislike which she showed toward him in future years dated from this episode.

More immediately, trouble for Penn again loomed with regard to Pennsylvania. For the time being, he had been upheld in his dispute with Lord Baltimore, but the faction in London which hoped to revoke all proprietary charters was still at work.

Pennsylvania's Charter appeared to be increasingly vulnerable to revocation. Crown agents stationed in the colonies, collaborating with the anti-proprietary elements in London, bombarded the authorities with reports that smuggling and piracy were rampant and violations of the Navigation Acts were commonplace. While these charges were exaggerated, they had some basis in fact. Penn accepted them at face value and sent repeated demands to the Council and Assembly for strict enforcement of the laws. For their parts, these bodies did little beyond making token gestures. Partly, this was because they knew that the situation was by no means as bad as it was being portrayed, and resented what they felt to be unfounded criticism. It is likely, too, that they did not appreciate the gravity of the threat to the Charter. In any case, Penn was too remote to take effective action and his strictures could be largely ignored. Frustrated, in November, 1686 Penn spoke openly of surrendering the colony to the King, and he did go so far as to write to the Council threatening to abolish the Frame of Government and take the power of absolute authority into his own hands.

Reports of the criticisms he had made to his colony's officials leaked to the court in London, where they were cited as admissions that the royal agents' charges were valid, and the belief grew that what Penn had called the "Holy Experiment" was merely a hypocritical cover for greed and corruption. As the year 1687 passed and Penn's instructions continued to have little effect, he created a five-man commission to exercise the executive powers formerly vested in the Council. This action not only offended the members of the Council but, as the men named to the new commission were all conservatives, it antagonized what had emerged, under the leadership of a lawyer named David Lloyd, as the dominant (and politically more radical) party in the Assembly.

By now, nearly five years had passed since the Frame of Government had been adopted, and the time was approaching when it was due to be submitted to London for review by the Privy Council. Considering the attitude toward Pennsylvania's popular government that had gained currency at court, Penn feared that under review the colony's laws would be assessed as being ineffective and therefore disallowed. Such a development would inevitably give added impetus to the movement to revoke the Charter. To forestall this eventuality, he hit on what seemed an ingenious solution and sent a request to the Council to act secretly to repeal all existing laws and then, also secretly, to reenact them, thereby gaining a five-year extension of the date by which they must be submitted for review. Whatever their views of the ethics of such a scheme, the members of the Council were sufficiently stung by their loss of executive authority that they refused to act on Penn's request.

Meanwhile, Philip Ford was pressing again for payment of the debt owing to him, which now had grown to 5,282 pounds. Penn responded that he could not lay his hands on such a sum in cash; he asked Ford for another two-year extension, at the end of which, he promised, he would pay six thousand pounds. As security, he gave Ford a mortgage on Pennsylvania in return for a rental of one peppercorn a year.

During all this period Penn continued to work for the rights of Protestant non-conformists. Even though he was not associated with efforts to defend the freedoms of persecuted Catholics, there were many who continued to believe that he was being used by James II as a tool to establish precedents which would open the door to toleration of Catholicism, with all the dangers which this was believed to entail.

Indeed, it was this fear of Catholicism which in late 1688 brought the bloodless revolution deposing James as King and bringing William of Orange and Mary to the throne as joint sovereigns of England. Firmly Protestant though they were, they represented the replacement of a King who was personally friendly and philosophically sympathetic to Penn with monarchs who at best viewed him with a degree of suspicion. His well-known friendship for James II and the persistent rumors that he was secretly a Catholic brought his arrest, in December, 1688, on the allegation that he was conspiring to commit treason. Although he was soon released, he was shortly in trouble again after he indiscreetly made a statement clearly indicating that he had been in correspondence with the exiled James, or at least with one of his close associates. Again he was released, but required to post a bond of six thousand pounds to assure that he would appear if he were ever summoned again. Through old friends in the confidence of the new King, Penn was able to secure the concession that he could remain free provided he refrained from any political activity. Nevertheless, in 1689 and 1690 Penn was periodically called in for questioning, although in each case he was soon released. Even some of his fellow Quakers began to believe that he was a Catholic, and to his unconcealed anger, on one occasion a delegation from one Quaker meeting was sent to question him outright concerning the matter.

At the same time, he did not actually break off his connection with James. On January 1, 1691, in fact, two letters from him to the former king were intercepted. They appeared to be innocent enough, but the possibility existed that they were written in code. On February 5, 1691, therefore, Queen Mary issued orders for him and a number of others to be apprehended on suspicion of treason against the Crown. Confronted with the evidence, Penn responded equivocally. Asked by the official who was investigating the matter to give an assurance that he had no information of any plot and would report any such information that might come into his hands, he replied that he would discuss the question only with the King and Queen, and then only if he were first given a guarantee of immunity.

Despite this peculiar stand, King William considered Penn to be harmless. He ruled that provided Penn retired completely to private life, remaining at home under periodic surveillance, and promised to report any knowledge of pro-Stuart activity which reached him, he would be subject to no further prosecution.

During all the time that Penn was encountering so much trouble in England he was being badgered by problems in Pennsylvania. Penn's talents lay in planning and theory rather than in practical administration, and many of these difficulties were largely of his own making.

King William III, after a painting by Sir Peter Lely, 1677 (courtesy, National Portrait Gallery, London).

Queen Mary II, after a painting by William Wissing. The date of the portrait is unknown (courtesy, National Portrait Gallery, London).

In 1688, he had appointed as Deputy Governor a non-Quaker, a former officer of Cromwell's army, Capt. John Blackwell. While Blackwell was known for scrupulous honesty in handling funds, he had no knowledge of Pennsylvania. His instructions from Penn were to see that a new Assembly and Council were elected, and then compelled to repeal all existing laws and reenact them—a process which, as noted above, the existing legislature had refused to carry out. As a lever to enforce cooperation, Penn told Blackwell to threaten that the Frame of Government would be canceled and all the privileges it prescribed would be withdrawn. Then, incredibly, having directed the Deputy Governor to take what amounted to an almost dictatorial stance, Penn wrote to the Council, saying that if it so recommended, Penn would dismiss Blackwell.

Even apart from the clashes which these conflicting instructions assured, the colonists were suspicious of Blackwell simply because he was a soldier and an outsider. It is not surprising that in short order both Blackwell and the Council were complaining bitterly to Penn against each other. Blackwell's attempts to follow Penn's orders to enforce the Navigation Acts angered the merchants, leading Blackwell to brand them as hypocrites, which offended them even more. His efforts to compel the legislature to obey Penn's instructions were seen as tyrannical, translating the quarrel from the level of personality to that of principle.

A new source of dissension arose when a rumor spread that a French and Indian expedition was about to attack the three lower counties and Blackwell called on the Council to organize a militia for defense. Such action was of course a violation of the principle of non-violence, and the Council took no step other than to warn the people against spreading false rumors. The three lower counties, which did not share Pennsylvania's pacifism and considered themselves vulnerable, felt betrayed, and existing sentiment for separation from Pennsylvania grew stronger.

Meanwhile, London was increasingly beginning to look on the British settlements in America not as a number of separate colonies but as a single entity whose elements should cooperate with each other, certainly in such matters as defense. When New York was threatened from Canada, therefore, the King called on Pennsylvania to contribute men and money for its protection. Both because of their principles and because they saw no threat to themselves, the Council was evasive when Blackwell asked them to act on this order. Soon after, Blackwell resigned in disgust.

This was only the beginning of a succession of disputes over the issue of military defense. The outbreak of war between France and England increased the prospect of French attack in America, so King William called on all British colonies to help New York. Again Pennsylvania's Council refused. This led the Lords Commissioners of Trade and Plantations to advise King William to cancel Penn's charter. While he stopped short of such drastic action, in October, 1692 he consolidated, for military purposes, all colonies from Maryland to Massachusetts into a single command under Benjamin Fletcher, who was already commander in New York. By so doing, he suspended Penn's authority to govern in Pennsylvania.

Penn had considerable reason to be annoyed with his colony. Hard-pressed financially, unable to collect his full income from Ireland, and failing to receive his quitrents from Pennsylvania, the debt to Philip Ford still unpaid and growing, his legal expenses mounting, he had asked that a hundred Philadelphians lend him a hundred pounds each, interest-free, for four years. His plea fell on deaf ears and he was compelled to live off capital by selling more of his lands in England. All the same, when Fletcher's appointment was announced, Penn promptly wrote to him warning him against exceeding the limits of his authority in Pennsylvania.

That authority was broad enough. In April, 1693, when Fletcher reached Philadelphia, he immediately proposed to dissolve the legislature, revoke existing laws, and intensify enforcement of the Navigation Acts. When the colonists protested, he revoked the Frame of Government and the Charter and announced that if they chose to place their loyalty to Penn ahead of their loyalty to the King, Pennsylvania would very likely be incorporated into Maryland or New York.

Under this pressure the Assembly offered a compromise. If Fletcher would recognize the Frame of Government the Assembly would vote him the 760 pounds he demanded. Even then, though, they would not vote it for military purposes; instead, they said that out of gratitude they were making a "free will" offering to William and Mary for the sovereigns to use as they might choose. Fletcher agreed to the terms but found that he had to wait for the money, which was raised by a property tax. As it turned out, many property owners evaded payment, little effort was made to collect the tax, and only about half the total was actually brought in.

The issue of Pennsylvania's military obligations, as perceived by the Crown, was by no means settled and would recur on an almost yearly basis. For Penn, this would pose an insoluble dilemma. Nonviolence was one of the cornerstones of his body of convictions. In 1693, he had published one of his most significant works, *An Essay Toward the Present and Future Peace of Europe,* which advocated establishment of an international parliament where disagreements could be settled through discussion instead of combat. If this was like so many of his ideas in being unattainable at the time, it was also like them in laying a foundation upon which future generations would build. But along with his sincere pacifism, he also was realist enough to see that open refusal to cooperate in any way with the Crown's military requests would virtually assure the establishment of complete royal control. Such control, he was confident, would impose much more extensive military obligations by decree. Each new instance, he seems to have reasoned, could best be dealt with at the time it developed.

During this period there was some improvement in his personal situation. In December, 1693, the surveillance under which he had been kept was formally lifted, leaving him free to move about. Whatever sense of relief he felt was soon blighted, however, for the health of his beloved wife, Gulielma, was rapidly declining, and on February 23, 1694, she died. Penn himself then suffered a period of serious illness from which he did not recover for several months.

In Pennsylvania at this stage Colonel Fletcher was announcing another requirement for military assistance on the threatened borders of New York. As it had done the year before, the Assembly enacted a tax, but this time with the proviso that the first four hundred pounds collected would be used for salaries for Pennsylvania officials; anything left over could be turned over to the Crown. Unsatisfactory as this was to Fletcher, to the authorities in London the Pennsylvanians appeared to be responding as dutiful subjects of the Crown. Penn seized the opportunity to petition the Lords Commissioners of Trade and Plantations for restoration of his Charter, and on August 20, 1694, his petition was approved, on the implied condition that when Fletcher declared a need for troops, Pennsylvania must supply and support her share.

In England, Penn had exercised his new freedom of movement to resume his active role as a Quaker preacher and administrator. Among the influential members of the Society of Friends was Thomas Callowhill, whom he often visited in Bristol. After one such visit, Penn began a correspondence with Callowhill's daughter, Hannah. Although she was at least twenty-four years his junior, in November, 1695 they announced their engagement and, on March

5 of the following year, were married. Throwing a damper on what was a happy event, however, was the death barely five weeks later of Penn's elder surviving son, Springett.

Although the age difference between Penn and his new wife caused some critical gossip, the union proved to be a happy one. Hannah quickly began relieving Penn of many troublesome burdens, not only taking over the responsibility for managing the household at Worminghurst but assisting her husband in other matters as well. As her father had trained her to administer his own commercial interests, she was able to complement the often unworldly Penn in practical affairs.

This is not to say that he did not continue to be troubled with financial problems. Pennsylvania was a source of persistent expenditures but of practically no income. Royal agents renewed their charges that the Deputy Governor, Penn's cousin, William Markham, who was again serving one of his several terms in that office, was incompetent if not corrupt. Markham denied these accusations and, on Penn's instructions, intensified his efforts to enforce the Navigation Acts and customs regulations, although often he received little local cooperation. The Lords Commissioners of Trade and Plantations launched an investigation with which, perversely, Penn refused to cooperate. Not until he was repeatedly summoned would he appear to testify, and when he finally made an appearance was formally rebuked for his attitude, although no steps were taken to deprive him of his colony.

Markham was having problems with the colonists as well as with the royal agents. On April 15, 1695, Colonel Fletcher had issued a call to Pennsylvania for eighty men and funds to support them, to reinforce New York's frontier defenses. The Assembly declared that eighty men could not be spared, then adjourned to preclude further argument. To the officials in England this looked like bad faith, but Penn explained that Pennsylvania was self-governing; as Proprietor, he therefore could only urge the colonists to comply with royal requests, he could not order them to do so. True as these statements were, to some they appeared evasive if not devious.

However, Penn did write to the Council, expressing the hope that it would try not to disappoint the King. This led the Council to vote a small sum—another "free will gift"—but the Assembly refused to agree unless Markham would grant a new Frame of Government greatly extending the powers of the Assembly.

Such a grant was not within the authority of a Deputy Governor, but the Assembly threatened that if he did not draw up a new

Hannah Callowhill Penn, a copy by John Hesselius about 1742 of an original portrait, now lost (courtesy, Historical Society of Pennsylvania).

Frame, they would enact their own version. Defeated, Markham drafted a constitution which greatly curtailed his own powers. By it, the Governor could make no fiscal, commercial or judicial decisions without the consent of the Council. The Assembly was made more powerful, being able now to initiate legislation and to meet and adjourn when it chose. The terms of this new Frame were to remain in effect until Penn personally disapproved it.

Although the establishment of an over-all military command for the American colonies as a whole had not been welcome, Penn saw the idea of unification in certain areas of activity as having considerable merit. In February, 1697, therefore, he submitted a proposal, "A Brief and Plain Scheme for Union," to provide for annual meetings of delegates from all the American colonies to resolve inter-colonial disagreements and to discuss matters of common interest. As the system was eventually elaborated, he saw it as being able to bring about facilitating inter-colonial trade, standardization of currency, adoption of mutually accommodating court procedures, cooperative repression of crime, and (by the establishment of a mint) even easing the perennial shortage of currency. The Lords Commissioners of Trade and Plantations, however, considered that London's position was stronger if the colonies could be dealt with individually, and Penn's scheme found little favor.

What with the dissension between provincial officials, the reported failure to take effective action against piracy and smuggling, and the consequently increased threat that the Lords Commissioners of Trade and Plantations might once again rescind the Proprietor's governmental authority, by 1698 it was becoming imperative for Penn to return to Pennsylvania to take personal charge of the situation. Many pressing problems in England remained to be settled, however, before he could again sail for America.

One of these concerned his surviving son, William, Jr., who was known as Billy. Although he was only seventeen, at this time he married Mary Jones, daughter of a Bristol merchant. As a wedding present, Penn gave Billy a copy of his new pamphlet in which he had collected over five hundred maxims, the product of his years of introspection and self-searching. Entitled *Fruits of Solitude*, it was meant to provide a comprehensive guide to what Penn believed to be the proper relations of a man with his fellows, his conscience and God. But, unlike his older brother, Springett, Billy was not attracted by the plain ways of the Quaker style of life, and was in fact something of a playboy. For this reason as well as because of his marriage, he was unwilling to leave England for what many considered a wilderness. As part of Billy's inheritance from his mother was Worminghurst, Penn and Hannah moved so that Billy's bride could be mistress in her new home. They lived for a time at Bath, then relocated at Bristol.

There was also the matter of Penn's still growing debt to Philip Ford. This financial relationship had become extremely complex through Ford's desire to avoid taxes on specie if he received a large cash settlement, and Penn's desire to protect his family from losing Pennsylvania if he were to be convicted of treason, which would have entailed attainder—that is, forfeiture of his property. Accordingly, some time earlier, Penn had "sold" Pennsylvania to Ford, who had then "leased" it back to Penn, who was to pay interest, or "rent," in terms of acreage. Ford thereby avoided a tax obligation and Penn avoided the risk of having his family's chief inheritance confiscated.

When Penn announced his plan to emigrate, Ford and his wife became concerned. Ford's health was poor, and his wife was worried about being able to collect what was due if her husband died before the matter was resolved. As tangled as the two men's affairs had become, trying to achieve settlement of debts to an estate rather than to a living man was certain to involve horrendous legal complications. Accordingly, Ford now demanded payment in full. There was no possibility that Penn could lay his hands on the thousands of pounds involved without selling much of the property which was his source of income. He agreed, therefore, to Ford's substitute proposal to redefine the lease of Pennsylvania in terms that would increase the sum coming to Ford. At Ford's request—prompted, he said, merely as a precaution—the new lease explicitly spoke of the payments as rent on the colony, implying that title had been transferred to Ford. Characteristically, Penn signed the agreement without reading it, or noting that it gave Ford extensive power of attorney.

Satisfied that his affairs were in good order, Penn boarded the *Canterbury* and sailed for Pennsylvania on September 8, 1699. Accompanying him this time were his wife, his daughter, Letitia, and his secretary, James Logan.

The Second Visit

The *Canterbury* reached Chester on November 30, 1699. Penn remained there only briefly, moving by barge with his family and secretary upriver to Philadelphia on December 3.

Eager as he must have been to see for himself the advances which had been made in the fifteen years he had been away, he found a number of developments which disturbed him. Philadelphia's population had grown to five thousand souls, outnumbered in British America only by Boston. The signs of prosperity were encouraging, but Penn feared that growing luxury might seduce the settlers from the ways of Quaker simplicity. The expansion of Philadelphia, moreover, had been achieved partly at the expense of some of the areas he had planned to keep open and uncrowded. Some sections were already deteriorating and were well on the way toward becoming slums.

There was much that required his personal attention, not the least being the need to demonstrate to the critics in London that he was taking a firm stand to assert control. Consequently, he temporarily abandoned his plan to settle at Pennsbury and rented a house in Philadelphia. Summoning the Council, before the month was out he issued a proclamation sternly condemning smuggling and piracy. He followed this up by obtaining restrictive laws aimed at making these crimes more difficult. All strangers and "suspicious characters" were required to explain who they were and why they had come to ferrymen and boatmen who brought them and to innkeepers who provided them with lodging. A night watch was established for Philadelphia, and regulations governing prices and standard weights of staples were issued. As time permitted, he made hasty visits to neighboring areas in New Jersey as well as Pennsylvania.

The latter part of January, 1700 brought the birth of the first child of his and Hannah's marriage to survive. Mother and baby, who was named John, were healthy, but the onset of winter weather brought a flare-up of Penn's gout, along with other ailments. These helped bring on an outlook toward matters in general that was almost testy.

Penn resented the refusal of the people of Pennsylvania to provide him with an income. From their point of view, having purchased the land from Penn they considered that they were freed from any further obligation to him, but he seems to have clung to an essentially feudal concept of himself as a magnate retaining perpetual rights as a sort of overlord. He was also annoyed with the authorities in London, who in his opinion should reimburse him for his out-of-pocket expenses for the government of the colony. Then, there was the matter of the Assembly.

Over the years, its membership had become divided into factions. Penn viewed political parties as a source of dissension, which was abhorrent. Furthermore, his thesis that men of good will would always make the right decisions meant that such dissension should be unnecessary. He had been able with little trouble to get legislation passed against smuggling and piracy, but he found that when it came to enforcing the laws, the legislators were much less compliant. The small success he realized in trying to bring the several political factions to unanimity led him to begin to wonder if the mass of people could indeed be relied upon to act as they should.

A particular troublemaker, to Penn's mind, was David Lloyd, who not only was the leader of the Assembly's more radical elements but also was the colony's Attorney General. Col. Robert Quary, the Crown official in charge of the Vice Admiralty court which handled cases involving violations of customs laws and the Navigation Acts, complained that Lloyd, whose duty it was to prosecute such cases, was in effect conniving with those accused to thwart the law. Penn was willing enough to suspend Lloyd from his office, but Lloyd continued to play his radical role in the Assembly.

In April, Penn and his family finally moved to Pennsbury. The elegant appointments of the mansion, the fine furnishings that had been brought from England, and the large staff of servants provided a life of considerable comfort, even luxury, compared with the standards prevailing for many of the colonists, although it differed little from the existence of a man of means to which Penn was accustomed. He entertained lavishly, including prominent In-

Pennsbury, reconstructed country home of William Penn, located in Bucks County.

dians as well as colonial dignitaries among his guests, living in a manner which he thought fitting to his position as Governor and Proprietor. There were those among the colonists, however, who considered his life style too ostentatious for a man who preached the virtues of Quaker austerity.

Always alert to promote human welfare, Penn addressed himself to the troubling problem of slavery. In principle, he considered it indefensible; in practice, however, he considered that slaves, as valuable property, had a better chance of being well treated than indentured servants. He also believed that some provision should be made to free slaves after a specified number of years and to furnish them with means of supporting themselves. With that in mind, he proposed that a six thousand-acre township be set aside for them, to be called Freetown. Once again, however, the Assembly proved to be an insurmountable obstacle and his plan had to be abandoned.

As the year 1701 progressed, Penn learned from friends in England that his charter was again in jeopardy, with a bill to eliminate all colonial proprietorships actually before Parliament. What had helped to bring this to a head had been a complaint that Penn, of all people, was condoning religious oppression of Church of England communicants in Pennsylvania.

This charge grew out of a recent law requiring banns to be posted for a month before a marriage could take place. Disregarding this law, an Anglican clergyman had performed a marriage ceremony for two servants. He was charged with the offense and brought to trial before a Quaker judge, who imposed a fine of twenty pounds. This was considered an excessive punishment, and other Anglicans took up the cry that they were being persecuted. Led by the rector of Christ Church in Philadelphia, they submitted a petition outlining their complaint to the Bishop of London.

Penn stated flatly that the law requiring the posting of the banns had not been initiated by him, although he considered that it provided a practical means of preventing bigamous marriages, and he thought that the fine was justified. Unconvinced, the Bishop referred the matter to the Board of Trade and Plantations with a request that the law be rescinded.

Compounding the situation was the Assembly's reaction to the latest request from the Crown for money to support the defenses of New York. The Assembly referred the request to Penn, asking for guidance as to the action it should take. Considering the fact that Pennsylvania was self-governing, Penn's response—that the request spoke for itself—is understandable even if it was not very helpful.

The Assembly replied that no money was available, and in any case it did not seem right for Pennsylvania to provide money when other colonies refused to do so. Penn's rejoinder was that he commended the request "to their serious thoughts and care." In what amounted to a form of attempted extortion, the Assembly implied that it would meet the request only if Penn made a number of concessions.

Penn angrily rejected this demand. All the same, he was willing to recognize that some elemental changes in the governmental structure were called for. Partly this was because the situation needed to be regularized: since 1695, the colony's government had actually been operating on a *de facto* basis; while Penn had tacitly accepted the Frame which the Assembly had compelled Governor Markham to grant, he had never officially approved it. Furthermore, at the same time that the Proprietor was not satisfied with some of its aspects, in other respects it had fallen short of what its proponents had hoped.

The new Frame of Government, which Penn completed on October 28, 1701, is known as the Charter of Liberties and remained as the basic law of Pennsylvania until the American Revolution.

The provision guaranteeing religious liberty was carried over from the previous constitutions. In other respects, however, considerable change was introduced. The Assembly alone, made up of four elected members from each county, now comprised the legislature. It would initiate, debate and pass or reject all laws. The Governor could veto its actions but could not prorogue or dissolve it. The Council was retained, but its members were not to be elected by the people but to be appointed by the Governor, in any number he chose. Its functions were no longer those of an upper legislative house but merely those of a consultative body. The religious liberty clause explicitly could never be altered, but any other portion of the Frame could be amended by a vote of six-sevenths of the Assembly, provided the Governor gave his approval. Recognizing the fact that the union with the three lower counties was not completely satisfactory, the Charter of Liberties contained a provision that after three years those counties could withdraw from Pennsylvania if they chose to do so; if they did dissolve the connection, the number of representatives from the Pennsylvania counties would be increased from four to eight.

The result was a structure which gave the Assembly the expanded role it had sought but which also strengthened the power of the Governor. Neither authority could impose its will on the other, but each could block the other's actions. If the law-making body could be considered more directly representative of the people, the Governor was in a position to keep it from going to extremes. Clearly, Penn had modified to a degree his earlier views concerning the ability of the general public to govern itself with prudence and wisdom, but he had created a balance which both liberal and conservative elements could accept as satisfactory.

This accomplished, he felt free to leave for England. To act as Governor during his absence he named Andrew Hamilton, who had considerable relevant experience from his services as Governor of both the Jerseys. As Penn's intention was to return to America as soon as he had dealt with the threat from London, he initially proposed to leave Hannah and his children at Pennsbury, but both his wife and daughter objected. Consequently, when on November 30 he sailed on the *Dalmahoy*, he was accompanied by his family. It was just as well, for he was never to return to Pennsylvania.

The Final Years

The remainder of Penn's life was marked by an almost unbroken succession of problems and disappointments.

The *Dalmahoy* made a rapid passage, and on December 31, 1701, Penn once again set foot on English soil. While Hannah and their son went to Bristol, Penn and Letitia hurried to London. It was fortunate that Letitia accompanied her father, for on the way he injured his gouty leg and despite her nursing was for weeks confined to a sick room. A development which boded no good for the future, although Penn would not have realized the implications at the time, was the death at this stage of his former steward, Philip Ford. As it was, the reports of the state of Penn's other affairs could not have aided his recovery.

Since the *Dalmahoy's* departure from Philadelphia, Robert Quary had submitted to London a list of complaints alleging inept administration and interference with the functioning of the Vice Admiralty court on the part of the Proprietor. What made the situation more ominous was that on March 8, William III died, to be succeeded by his sister-in-law, Anne. She was the second daughter of James II and, like her elder sister, Mary, had been brought up on strictly Anglican lines in order to counteract popular objection to her father's Catholicism. Apart from the uncertainty accompanying any change of monarchs, Queen Anne had a reputation for being strongly opposed to religious non-conformity. Even though Hannah gave birth to another son, Thomas, on the day after the King died, Penn did not dare leave London to be with her at Bristol. He feared now not only for his continued proprietorship of Pennsylvania but for the future of the Society of Friends itself. There seemed to be a real possibility that the oppression from which religious dissenters had been free for a decade would reappear.

To try to forestall such a development, on behalf of the Society of Friends Penn drew up a memorial expressing the loyalty of "the people commonly called Quakers" to the new Queen and begging her toleration. This step proved to be wise. Queen Anne promised to preserve the Act of Toleration and informed Penn that "you and your friends may be assured of my protection."

If the future of the Quakers seemed secured, the problem with the Lords Commissioners of Trade and Plantations remained unsettled. Preoccupied as he had been with his health, the Society of Friends, and his family affairs, Penn had been dilatory—some thought him evasive or intentionally unresponsive—to the questions from the Lords Commissioners which stemmed from Robert Quary's charges. Hoping that the effects of these criticisms would have died away, he also postponed until June 22 any action to carry out the requirement, specified in the Charter, to obtain the sovereign's approval of his nomination of Andrew Hamilton as Deputy Governor. Instead of achieving the results Penn had sought, his delayed submission of the nomination was interpreted as deliberate flouting of the royal authority. The Privy Council, acting in the Queen's name, did eventually grant approval, but only on the basis of a number of restrictive conditions: Hamilton's appointment was to be probationary for one year, and only then if Penn posted a bond of two thousand pounds for Hamilton's good behavior; if he agreed to answer promptly, in writing, the questions to which he had hitherto been so dilatory in replying; and if he made an explicit statement that the Queen's confirmation of Hamilton did not affect such claims as she might have to the three lower counties.

Penn's personal affairs also were troubled.

There was the matter of the debt to Philip Ford. In violation of a promise he had made to Penn, Ford had included in his will a reference to his "title" to Pennsylvania, specifying that unless within six months Penn paid the sums due—stated to be over eleven thousand pounds—Ford's interest in the colony should be sold for the benefit of his heirs. In April, Ford's widow, Bridget, confronted Penn with a demand that he pay his debt. Dismayed at what he considered Ford's bad faith, Penn agreed to pay the "rents" that were owing, but stipulated that it must be clearly understood that title of

Pennsylvania had never been transferred and that the accounts would be submitted for his examination and rejection of any errors that might be found. Realizing that the problems were serious, he retained attorneys to guide him in the matter.

Then, there was the matter of Letitia's marriage. Her prospective husband was a widower named William Aubrey, a London merchant. He was demanding a large marriage settlement. When Penn offered to provide it in the form of Pennsylvania lands, Aubrey said that this was unacceptable and demanded two thousand pounds in cash. Unable to lay his hands on such a sum, Penn finally agreed to sign a note for that amount, paying ten per cent in annual interest, with the principal being due in full six months after any interest payment fell into arrears. Subsequently, in August, shortly before the wedding was to take place, an acquaintance from Philadelphia, William Masters, appeared with the claim that he and Letitia had been formally engaged. As he could produce no proof, Letitia and Aubrey were duly married, but not until after considerable worry and gossip.

In Pennsylvania, Andrew Hamilton had been plunged into disputes with the Assembly, chiefly over the perennial question of responding to royal requests for money to help defend New York from French attack. Despite Hamilton's efforts, the Assembly stubbornly refused to raise money for New York, or even to organize a militia or build forts for Pennsylvania's defense. Penn feared that the whole survival of his administration might again be challenged and offered to pay from his own funds the 350 pounds requested. This gesture, which proved to be unnecessary when the Governor of New York reported that the danger had subsided and he no longer needed military assistance, nonetheless was of benefit to Penn's standing at court. He failed to take advantage of this beneficially altered view, however, and reverted to his former attitude of evasiveness and delay toward the requests of the Board of Trade and Plantations.

In an effort to ease his financial problems and to force the colony to assume the costs of its own government, he pressured James Logan, who was now Secretary of the Province and Clerk of the Council, to obtain new taxes and collect the quitrents that were due. Logan loyally and energetically tried to meet Penn's requests. As usual, the Assembly proved willing to enact taxes but, also as usual, it would do nothing to enforce collection. In all fairness, Pennsylvania and the American colonies in general suffered from a continuing shortage of currency, with most commerce taking the form of barter. To counter this situation, Penn and Logan tried to work out a system whereby payment could be made with products to be sold in England, but the scheme yielded little profit when one ship was lost with all its cargo and another shipment was mishandled by the agents to whom it had been entrusted.

A new problem arose when Andrew Hamilton died, raising the requirement for Penn to name a replacement as Deputy Governor. Unwisely, he proposed to reappoint William Markham, who had been thoroughly discredited in the eyes of the London authorities by Robert Quary's numerous allegations. Penn's suggestion, in fact, was considered not only unacceptable but offensive.

Having grown more and more discouraged, on May 11, 1703 Penn submitted a petition to the Lords Commissioners of the Board of Trade and Plantations, proposing to resign his control of the government of Pennsylvania to the Crown for an unspecified sum of money, provided that the laws and civil rights that had been established there were preserved and that he be allowed to retain certain of his privileges. This aroused considerable interest among the Lords Commissioners, who asked him to be more precise concerning what he had in mind. The reply he eventually made stipulated a price of forty thousand pounds and a list of privileges which, in some eyes, would leave him with his special status as Proprietor unchanged in many essentials. From the Crown's viewpoint, the proposal was completely unacceptable, and although negotiations continued sporadically over many months, the matter ultimately was dropped.

Meanwhile, Hamilton's replacement still had to be named, so Penn secured approval for the appointment of John Evans to be Deputy Governor not only of Pennslyvania but, separately, of the three lower counties, which under the terms of the Charter of Liberties had decided to become an independent colony under their own assembly. Of the many unfortunate appointments Penn made, this was to prove among the worst. Evans was only twenty-six years old, lacking maturity as well as administrative experience. He knew nothing of colonial affairs in general, not to mention the special conditions prevailing in Pennsylvania, and if he had no feeling against Quakers and their beliefs he also had no particular sympathy for them.

During 1703, Hannah had been living at her father's house at Bristol, and there on July 30 Hannah Margaret, the third child of Penn's second marriage, was born. In October, when the baby was old enough to travel safely, Hannah wrote to her husband asking if she and the children could join him at London. Much as he wished to be reunited with his family permanently instead of being limited to the short visits he managed from time to time, he had to reply that his lodgings were not suitable for so many and that as matters stood financially, he could not for the moment find adequate housing in London that he could afford to rent. Within the next few months, however, he did succeed in locating a residence, and there he was soon joined by Hannah and the three children.

In the meantime, his eldest son, Billy, had been a subject of recurrent concern. He was an amiable young man but he lacked the depth his father had tried to develop in him. The sober Quaker way did not appeal to him and he was attracted to the bright social life of a wealthy young gentleman of fashion. Extravagant to the point of fecklessness, he continually piled up heavy debts which his father had to pay. Penn was distressed, but he was unable to accept his son's limitations. Rather fatuously, he convinced himself that a taste of responsibility was all that was needed to cause Billy to face up to his obligations and accept the role visualized for him. To provide this, he decided to send the young man to Pennsylvania. Late in the year, therefore, leaving his own wife and children behind, Billy sailed with John Evans for Philadelphia, arriving on February 2, 1704.

For the next several months until the early fall of 1704, when Penn, Hannah, and the younger children returned to Bristol, Penn seems for once to have been able to lead an untroubled existence. But then disturbing reports concerning Billy and Governor Evans began to reach him.

Apart from the fact that the Pennsylvanians had resented the appointment of so young a Governor, Evans promptly began clashing with members of the Assembly. When he had relayed to them New York's yearly request for military assistance, Penn learned, they had asserted that steady expansion of settlement had now given Pennsylvania its own Indian frontier to guard. If that was the case, Evans had replied, Pennsylvania should have its own militia. On his own authority he formed a force of unpaid volunteers which he named the Governor's Guard. To the scandal of the peace-loving Quakers, Billy became the drill-master of the organization. Non-Quaker elements of the population became equally annoyed, if for different reasons. For one thing, on July 11 Evans granted members of the Guard exemption from serving the stints of duty with the city's night watch to which all Philadelphia citizens were obligated. Non-Philadelphians, even though not subject to watch duty, also had objections to the militia, seeing it as an instrument through which the Governor might impose his will on the Assembly by force.

Worse was to come. In August, the resentments that had grown up gave rise to an unseemly tavern brawl between some militiamen — among whom Billy figured prominently — and the members of the watch, which almost led to the would-be soldiers being brought into court on charges of disorderly conduct. The charges were dropped but the scandal spread like wildfire. Nor was this the end of Billy's revels, and it must have been especially trying to Penn when not only James Logan but his old antagonist, David Lloyd, wrote gloomy news of the straits to which the excesses of the Proprietor's prospective heir were bringing the Province. By the time Penn decided that he had no choice but to bring his son back to England, Billy had anticipated him and on his own initiative had taken ship from New York. In January, 1705, after less than a year abroad, he appeared at Worminghurst. Having long ago broken from the Quakers in spirit, he now notified his father that he was formally abandoning any affiliation with the Society of Friends.

The birth of another daughter, Margaret, in the preceding November had provided Penn with another reminder of the financial requirements he must somehow meet if all his children were to be provided for in a suitable manner. Perhaps it was the combination of financial concerns and distress over Billy which brought on the illness which afflicted him at this time. He described it as a fever, but it may have been a mild stroke. Although he soon recovered, his state of mind could not have been helped when, in March, Billy announced that he planned to stand for Parliament; this meant that, if elected, he would have to violate the Quaker prohibition against swearing oaths and, in his father's view, thereby put his very soul in jeopardy. As it happened, Billy was not elected, but Penn seems to have realized that Billy's break with the precepts under which he had been brought up was now complete.

Billy's next scheme was to seek a career as a soldier. Penn, always the indulgent father, despite the inconsistency this time with his principles as a Quaker, used all the influence he could muster to help his son. He was offended, moreover, when the best offer that materialized was an appointment as a captain in an Irish regiment, and indignantly rejected it as being unworthy of a man of Billy's birth and standing.

Continuing complaints from Pennsylvania were making the error committed in appointing Evans increasingly clear. Robert Quary informed the Board of Trade and Plantations that the Deputy

Governor did nothing to control vice and crime. Others relayed stories that Evans was associating with men and women of lurid reputation and that his visits to the Indians were nothing but excuses for debauchery. Penn reprimanded his Deputy Governor for his misbehavior, but was unable to find valid grounds for dismissing him outright.

As if all this were not enough, Bridget Ford and her children again pressed their demands for payment. Analyzing the accounts, Penn and his lawyers had found that these contained numerous claims that were clearly fraudulent. Ford had charged excessive interest, he had omitted credits which should have been entered, and he had imposed outrageously unreasonable agent's fees for transactions he had carried out. Instead of the fourteen thousand pounds the Fords now claimed as due, Penn's attorneys held that the total he owed was only 4,303 pounds, and this he offered to pay. Unfortunately for this offer, in 1697 he had signed a note acknowledging his debt at that time as being 6,334 pounds, so the Fords predictably refused to accept this proposal. Instead, they filed suit for the staggering sum of twenty thousand pounds. By a succession of legal maneuvers, Penn's attorneys were able to delay the case being heard, but it still hung over his head. The one happy event while all this was going on was that in January, 1706, Hannah bore another son, Richard.

The problems in Pennsylvania acquired a new twist when David Lloyd began proceedings aimed at impeaching Penn's faithful supporter, James Logan. The charges had no foundation, but merely airing them was damaging. For once, Evans proved to be an asset, for he contended that the Deputy Governor and the Council had no authority to hear a case of impeachment. This enabled him to block any further action.

Although Penn was preoccupied during most of the year with trying to deal with successive stages of the Fords' lawsuit, he did give considerable thought to his children's future security. After the birth of another son, Dennis, in February, 1707, he made a proposal to Billy. Under the laws of primogeniture, Billy was heir to all his father's lands in Ireland. Primogeniture had been explicitly banned in Pennsylvania, so Penn's rights there would be divided equally among his sons. Now he asked Billy to relinquish his claims to the Irish estates in favor of the younger children, receiving in return two-thirds of Pennsylvania. Billy did not commit himself, but the possibility remained open.

In a more immediate sense, both men had urgent bills to pay, and before the year was out they agreed to sell the rights they shared in Worminghurst. This helped alleviate their situation in the short term. Also, Evans finally overstepped himself. Personally chasing a ship which had left Philadelphia without filing the clearance papers required, he had boarded her where she had taken refuge in a New Jersey port. This infringement of another colony's jurisdiction was not only blatant but particularly impolitic because present in the port was the Governor of New Jersey (now a royal colony), who was no less a personage than a cousin of Queen Anne. Summary dismissal of Evans was mandatory for reasons of expedience, but it is likely that Penn welcomed the opportunity that had been presented.

Late in November, the Fords' lawsuit finally came up for a ruling. With accounts so tangled over so many years, the court was unwilling to try to trace its way through the whole record but confined itself to the basic and indisputable facts that Penn had given Ford a deed to his colony as security and then had failed to pay the "rents" that were due. Left unsettled was the question of the amount owed, but the fact remained that Penn was clearly vulnerable to imprisonment in the Fleet, the debtors' prison. Penn chose to stand on principle, contending that he owed no such sum as the Fords demanded and would go to debtors' prison if he must.

The Fords took him at his word. On January 7, 1708, while he was attending meeting, bailiffs entered the building with an order for his immediate arrest. His attorneys, who were present, protested at the indignity which was threatened to a man of his age and standing. They prevailed on the bailiffs to leave, promising that Penn would surrender himself voluntarily before the day was out.

Penn was not actually jailed but was required only to remain within the vicinity of the Fleet. He found comfortable lodgings, although he had to endure the heartbreaking experience of being unable to be with Hannah while their little daughter, Hannah Margarita, was dying at Bristol. He was able to find some escape from his grief, however, in dealing with his business and administrative affairs, appointing a Deputy Governor—Charles Gookin—to replace Evans and taking necessary steps to counter the Fords' further persecution.

In fact, by their intransigence in refusing the compromises that had been offered, and particularly by their high-handed action in trying to have Penn dragged as a prisoner from the meetinghouse itself, they had antagonized non-Quakers as well as Friends. Failing to recognize how they had made Penn a sympathetic figure, in

February they capped their previous mishandling of their case by petitioning the Queen to grant them a new charter to Pennsylvania, contending that the government of the colony should be a concomitant of the deed to its ownership. The request was heard by the Lord Chancellor, who gave it short shrift, pointing out that Penn and his heirs still had the right to redeem the deed to Pennsylvania; if they exercised that right, transferring the government now would merely require it to be returned later.

Thus thwarted, the Fords finally decided on a more reasonable approach, offering to accept seventy-six hundred pounds as payment in full, on condition that three thousand pounds of that sum be paid at once. Penn's friends immediately formed a consortium to begin raising the money, which Penn would secure with mortgages on Pennsylvania acreage — not, this time, on the Province itself. Meanwhile, Hannah had joined her husband in his lodgings near the prison; and there, on September 5, shortly before the debt was paid and Penn released from restraint, what was to be their last child, named Hannah for her mother, was born. She was a sickly infant, however, and survived only until January 24, 1709.

It was shortly after this sad event that Penn's wife and children went back to her father's house at Bristol while Penn, freed now from the long-drawn-out dispute with the Fords, returned to his active religious work. Throughout the remainder of 1709 into the early part of the following year, he spent much of his time traveling and preaching through England. Only in February, 1710 was he reunited with his family, establishing a residence at Ruscumbe, in Berkshire. Billy and his family for a time shared the household, so that except for Letitia and her husband, Penn's entire family was collected under one roof.

During this period he renewed his efforts to sell his proprietary rights in Pennsylvania to the Crown. Governor Gookin, like his predecessors, was finding himself embroiled in disputes with the Assembly, which was continuing to seek to extend its powers into areas which Gookin (and Penn as well) considered to be properly within the purview of the executive. On another level, Penn continued to be disappointed at not receiving from the colony the revenues which he believed to be his moral if not his legal due. All in all, he was ready now to cut his losses and rid himself of what he had come to view as nothing but a source of continuing exasperation and heavy expense.

By February, 1711, agreement with the royal authorities seemed to be coming closer. Penn had lowered his price to twenty thousand pounds, to be paid over a period of seven years, and the Lords Commissioners of the Board of Trade and Plantations formally recommended to the Queen that his terms be met. Such matters took considerable time, however, and more than a year passed before the next step occurred. The Queen's advisers, believing that Penn was unwilling or unable to hold out for the price he had named, in June, 1712 made a counter-offer to buy Pennsylvania for twelve thousand pounds paid over four years. Their reasoning proved to be perceptive, for Penn accepted their offer, provided that a thousand pounds of the purchase price should be paid to him immediately.

The fine details still had to be worked out, and that occupied more months. In the meantime, having collected the advance, Penn and Hannah made a visit to Bristol. There, on October 4, Penn suffered a severe stroke. This not only left him partially paralyzed but affected his mind. Although he made a considerable recovery, he remained weak, and his physicians advised Hannah to keep all matters of business from him. One consequence was that the conclusion of the sale of the colony had to be suspended, at least for the time being. As matters turned out, it was never to be completed.

The Penns remained at Bristol until late January, 1713, while Penn regained enough strength to return to London. Once there, he tried to pick up his former activities. This quickly proved to be impossible, so he traveled to the rural quiet of Ruscumbe. Short as the journey was, it turned out to be too great a strain, and immediately upon his arrival he suffered a relapse which left him not only greatly weakened but unable to concentrate and subject to lapses of memory. From time to time, he could leave his house to attend meeting, but even these occasions were relatively rare.

During this time, the Crown had not lost interest in acquiring Pennsylvania as a royal colony, and in March, 1714 repeated the offer of twelve thousand pounds. The problem was that Penn could no longer be considered legally competent to consent to the sale. The authorities then suggested that they would consider it acceptable if Hannah, even though she did not have a power of attorney, would guide her husband's hand in a signature on a deed of transfer. Regardless of the questionable legality of such a procedure, she was willing to adopt it, as she knew that up to the moment of his disabling illness, Penn had fully intended to complete the transaction. At this, however, there were objections from Billy and his brother-in-law, William Aubrey, as well as from several of the men who held mortgages on Pennsylvania lands as security for the sums they

Philadelphia at about the time of Penn's death, painted by Peter Cooper (courtesy, Library Company of Philadelphia).

had collected to pay the Fords. These protests put an end to the matter, and it became necessary to repay the thousand pounds that had been advanced in 1712.

Still hoping that her husband might recover, at least in some degree, Hannah took him in the summer of 1715 to the health resort at Bath. The trip was not too hard on him, but the waters had no curative effect and the two returned to Ruscumbe, whose vicinity Penn was never to leave again.

So far as handling the issues which continued to come from Pennsylvania for the Proprietor's rulings, Hannah now took over, governing the colony in her husband's name with good sense and sound judgment. In 1716 she dismissed Gookin as Deputy Governor, replacing him with William Keith, a man who combined considerable experience as an administrator with an unusual ability to bring about cooperation between competing elements. This proved to be perhaps the best appointment the colony had yet seen.

During these years, Penn's health underwent a slow but steady decline. When he was not semi-conscious, he showed a happy but child-like attitude, not clearly aware of his surroundings and often failing to recognize the old friends who visited him. He continued in this manner, growing steadily weaker, until finally, early on the

Jordan's Friends Meeting House, Buckinghamshire, burial place of William Penn and members of his family.

morning of July 30, 1718, he died peacefully. He was buried in the graveyard adjacent to Jordan's Friends Meeting House, lying beside the grave of his first wife and near those of many of his children.

By his will, half of Pennsylvania went to his son John, the remaining half being divided equally between the other three sons of his second marriage. Billy's inheritance was the Irish estates, although with these went the title of Proprietor of Pennsylvania. Dissatisfied, he filed suit, claiming the entire colony under the law—inapplicable in Pennsylvania—of primogeniture. A finding on his claim was not handed down until 1726, by which time Billy himself had been dead for six years. Hannah died in 1726, only days after the case was settled, and her youngest son, Dennis, survived her only a short time. This left the proprietorship being shared by her three surviving sons, John, Thomas, and Richard, remaining in their hands or those of their heirs until the American Revolution relegated it to the past.

Conclusion

William Penn can be looked at as a religious thinker and publicist, as a political theorist, as a colonial administrator, or as a man with human worries and human foibles. To focus on any one of these facets in isolation from the others, however, is artificial, for each had its effect on, and was affected by, the rest. Penn's views on individual liberty, for example, were clearly nothing more than an application to political relationships of his convictions concerning religious freedom of conscience. His profound belief that in spiritual matters each man can know the truth if he earnestly search his heart carried over into the thesis that in a temporal matter the only requirement for determining the wise course of action is for good people to consider that matter with complete honesty.

Perhaps it was because this political philosophy was rooted in religious conviction that Penn was so offended by those who tried to reshape according to their own preferences the courses which Pennsylvania followed. His belief in religious toleration did not mean that he agreed that there could be different ideas of truth, but only that in spiritual matters all people had the right to be wrong. Penn himself saw truth as absolute, whether it was religious or political. Since for his part he conscientiously determined what was truth in any given case, any who differed from him could do so only because they had not sought earnestly for an answer or because, while knowing what was right, they perversely and wickedly opposed its pursuit. It followed, therefore, that Penn saw his political opponents not merely as being in error but as being evil men. This viewpoint, even apart from the style of disputation prevailing at the time, led Penn in his published arguments and his more contentious correspondence to devote as much space to abusive, personal assaults upon those who differed with him as to the weaknesses of the views they were trying to advance. One result was a relationship between Proprietor and colonial government which was seldom harmonious and sometimes openly hostile.

With this, Penn was manifestly unsuccessful as a manager of practical affairs and overly trusting, even naive, when it came to judging character. Too many of the men he appointed to high office had no pertinent experience, and were chosen because of virtues Penn saw (or thought he saw) which he valued but which had no relevance to effectiveness in administration. Even with the best will in the world, several of the governors he named found themselves charged with carrying out conflicting instructions, and at times actually being undercut, in effect, by the Proprietor himself in their relations with the other branches of the colony's government. Apart from these avoidable difficulties, Penn never comprehended that he was trying to combine elements which inherently could not blend: having put government in the hands of the people to a degree that was generations ahead of its time, he was trying to impose on this ultramodern, basically democratic government a paternalistic economic system which was essentially feudal. The two were incompatible, and conflict and dissension were unavoidable.

There can be little doubt that in his own mind, Penn would have considered his work in the religious field to be of far more lasting importance than what he had done to influence political thought and to apply his thinking in establishing what became with astonishing rapidity a flourishing colony. Indeed, the example he set as a man of principle, regardless of the legal consequences to himself, undoubtedly brought adherents to his views and certainly won eventual sympathy from many who had been his oppressors. His unfailing championship of the rights of all dissenting sects, not just those of his fellow Quakers, was a significant factor in the eventual relaxation of the repressive laws aimed at non-conformists.

There can also be little doubt, however, that the lines along which Pennsylvania developed brought him many disappointments and, in some respects, a degree of disillusionment. Nevertheless, despite the fact that his ideals were not realized to the degree he had hoped, it is in the field of political theory—admittedly derived in substantial respects from his religious convictions—that Penn's influence perhaps had its most sweeping effect. Imperfect though the result may have been in his eyes, the fact remains that in the process of creating a colony where men enjoyed the broadest individual freedom yet known, he laid the foundations for what became some of the most fundamental guiding principles of an entire nation. Not only Pennsylvania but America as a whole owes him a lasting debt.

Suggestions for Further Reading

BEATTY, EDWARD C. O. *William Penn as Social Philosopher.* New York: Columbia University Press, 1939. Reprint available, New York: Octagon Books, 1972.

BRONNER, EDWIN B. *William Penn's Holy Experiment: The Founding of Pennsylvania, 1681-1701.* New York: Columbia University Press, 1962. Reprint available, Westport, Conn.: Greenwood Press, 1978.

BRONNER, EDWIN B. and FRASER, DAVID. *The Papers of William Penn.* Vol. 5. *William Penn's Published Writings, 1660-1726: An Interpretive Bibliography.* Philadelphia: University of Pennsylvania Press, 1986.

BURANELLI, VINCENT. *The King and the Quaker: A Study of William Penn and James II.* Philadelphia: University of Pennsylvania Press, 1962.

DOLSON, HILDEGARDE. *William Penn, Quaker Hero.* New York: Random House, 1961. Available for readers grades 3 to 7.

DUNN, MARY MAPLES. *William Penn: Politics and Conscience.* Princeton: Princeton University Press, 1967.

DUNN, MARY MAPLES and RICHARD S., genl. eds. *The Papers of William Penn.* Vols. 1-4. Philadelphia: University of Pennsylvania Press, 1981-1987.

DUNN, RICHARD S. and MARY MAPLES, eds. *The World of William Penn.* Philadelphia, University of Pennsylvania Press, 1986.

ENDY, MELVIN, *William Penn and Early Quakerism.* Princeton: Princeton University Press, 1973.

FOSTER, GENEVIEVE. *The World of William Penn.* New York: Charles Scribner's Sons, 1973. For younger readers.

ILLICK, JOSEPH E. *William Penn the Politician: His Relations with the English Government.* Ithaca: Cornell University Press, 1967.

NASH, GARY B. *Quakers and Politics: Pennsylvania, 1681-1776.* Princeton: Princeton University Press, 1968.

PEARE, CATHERINE OWENS. *William Penn.* Philadelphia: J. B. Lippincott, 1956.

SODERLUND, JEAN R., ed. *William Penn and the Founding of Pennsylvania, 1680-1684.* Philadelphia: University of Pennsylvania Press, 1983. Selected writings and correspondence of the founder, available in cloth and paper bindings.

VINING, ELIZABETH GRAY. *William Penn, Mystic, as Reflected in His Writings.* Wallingford, Pa.: Pendle Hill Publications, 1969. May be purchased from the publisher.

WILDES, HARRY EMERSON. *William Penn.* New York: Macmillan, 1974.

Index

Act of Conformity, 9
Act of Toleration, 59
Admiralty, British, 9
America, 23-25, 27, 33, 72
American Revolution, 57, 70
Amyraut, Moïse, 10-11
Anne, Queen of England, 58-59, 65-67
Arran, Earl of, 14
Aubrey, William, 60, 66-67

Baltimore, Lord, 29, 35-37, 39-40, 43
Bath, 53, 69
Berkeley, John, Lord, 24
Billinge, Edward. See Byllinge, Edward
Blackwell, *Capt.* John, 47
Board of Trade and Plantations, 39-40, 48-50, 52, 56, 59-61, 63, 67
Boston, Mass., 54
Brief Account of the Province of Pennsylvania, A, 30
"Brief and Plain Scheme for Union, A," 52
Bristol, 20, 49, 52-53, 58-59, 61-62, 65-67
Buckinghamshire, 2, 20
Bucks County, Pa., 35
Bushell, Edward, 22
Byllinge, Edward, 24-25

Callowhill, Hannah. See Penn, Hannah (Callowhill)
Callowhill, Thomas, 49-50, 61, 66
Cambridge University, 9
Canada, 47
Canterbury (ship), 53
Carrickfergus, Mutiny at, 14
Catholics, Catholicism, 2, 4, 21, 24, 26-27, 40, 44-45, 58
Charles I, 2, 4, 6, 11
Charles II, 2, 6, 13, 21, 23-24, 26-27, 29, 36, 39-40
Charter of Liberties, 57, 61
Chester, Pa., 34-35, 53
Chester County, Pa., 34
Chigwell Free School, 5
Christ Church (Oxford), 8-9
Christ Church (Philadelphia), 56

Church of England, 1, 8, 13, 18, 23, 30, 56, 58
Civil War, English, 2, 4
Clarendon Code, 8-9, 13
Colonies, British, 1, 29-30, 37, 40, 43, 47-48, 52, 54, 56, 60
Commons, House of, 26
"Concessions and Agreements," 25
Constitution, United States, 25
Conventicle Act, 13, 21
Cork, 5-6, 16, 20
Corporation Act, 8
Council, Pennsylvania Provincial, 32, 35-36, 43-44, 47-48, 50, 52, 54, 57, 64
Cromwell, Oliver, 4-6, 47
Crown authority, 13, 18, 23, 25-27, 29, 39, 45, 48-49, 56, 61, 66-67

Dalmahoy (ship), 58
Deal, 34
Declaration of Indulgence, 23
Delaware. See "Three Lower Counties"
Delaware Indians, 35
Delaware River, 27, 29, 33-34, 39
Dover, 6
Dublin, 14, 20
Dutch (see also Holland), 30

Endeavour (ketch), 39
Essay Toward the Present and Future Peace of Europe, An, 49
Europe, 4, 6, 11, 30-31
Evans, John, 61-65

Fenwick, John, 24-25, 31
"Fifth Monarchists," 9, 16-17
First Frame of Government, 32-33, 35
"First Purchasers," 31
Five Mile Act, 13, 22
Fleet Prison, 65
Fletcher, *Col.* Benjamin, 48-50
Ford, Bridget, 53, 59, 64-66, 69
Ford, Philip, 20, 42, 44, 48, 53, 58-59
Foundations of God Standeth, The, 18
Fox, George, 23-25, 42
France, French, 10-11, 21, 30-31, 39, 47-48, 60

73

Freetown, 56
Friends, Society of. See Quakers
Fruits of Solitude, 52

General Assembly, Pennsylvania, 32, 35-37, 42-44, 47-50, 52, 54-57, 60, 62-63, 66
Germantown, Pa., 36
Germany, Germans, 23, 25, 30-31, 36
"Glorious Revolution." See Revolution of 1688
Gookin, Charles, 65-66, 69
Government (see also William Penn, politics and government; Pennsylvania, government), 25, 29-33, 35-36
Great Case of Liberty of Conscience, The, 22-23
Great Law, The, 35

Hamilton, Andrew, 58-61
Hispaniola, 5
Holland, 4, 11, 13, 21, 23, 25, 30, 43
Holy Experiment, 44

Indians, 20, 35, 37, 47, 55-56, 62, 64
Innocency with Its Open Face: An Apology for Sandy Foundations Shaken, 18
Inns of Court, 11
Ireland, Irish, 2, 4-5, 14, 16, 20, 31, 36, 42, 48, 63-64, 70
Italy, 11

Jamaica, 5
James II, 6, 11, 13, 24, 26-27, 29, 33, 35, 39-40, 42-45, 58
Jenkins, *Sir* Leoline, 27
Jesuits, 18, 26
Jones, Mary. See Penn, Mary (Jones)
Jordan's Friends Meeting House, 70

Keith, William, 69
Kent County, Delaware, 35
Kinsale, 6, 14, 16
Krefeld, 36

Lincoln's Inn, 11, 13-14
Lloyd, David, 44, 55, 63-64
Loe, Thomas, 5-6, 16
Logan, James, 53, 60-61, 63-64

London (see also Crown authority), 2, 4, 8-11, 13, 17, 20-21, 29-30, 39, 42-43, 47, 49, 52, 54, 58-62, 67
London, Bishop of, 18, 56
Long Island, New York, 35
Lords, House of, 26
Lowestoft, Battle of, 13, 17
Lowther, Anthony, 16

Macroom, 5-6
Markham, William, 30, 50, 52, 57, 61
Mary II, 43-45, 48, 58
Maryland, 27, 29, 37, 39, 48
Massachusetts, 48
Masters, William, 60
Mead, William, 21-22
Mediterranean Sea, 2, 4
Militia, Military, 30, 37, 39, 47-50, 52, 56, 60, 62-63
Minety, Gloucs., 2
Monmouth, Duke of, 40
Monmouth's Rebellion, 40
Munster, 17

Navigation Acts, 39-40, 43, 47-48, 50, 55
Navy, Parliamentary, 2
Navy Commission, 4, 6, 14, 17
New Castle, Del., 29, 34
New Castle County, Delaware, 35
New Jersey (see also West Jersey), 24, 54, 58, 65
New York, 27, 35, 47-50, 56, 60, 62-63
Newgate Prison, 21-23, 32
No Cross, No Crown, 18, 20, 33
Nonconformists, 21, 23, 25, 39, 42, 44, 58, 71

Oates, Titus, 26
Oaths, 18, 22-23, 26, 40, 63
Ormonde, Duke of, 14
Orrery, Earl of, 17
Owen, *Dr.* John, 9-10
Oxford University, 8-9, 11

Paris, 10-11
Parliament, 2, 4, 6, 8-9, 21, 24-26, 30, 40, 42-43, 56, 63
Pastorius, Francis Daniel, 36

74

Penington, Isaac, 20
Penn, Dennis, 64, 70
Penn, Giles, 2
Penn, Gulielma Maria (Springett), 20, 23-24, 33-34, 42, 49, 53, 70
Penn, Hannah (Callowhill), 49-50, 53-54, 58-59, 61-62, 64-67, 69-70
Penn, Hannah (daughter of the Proprietor), 66
Penn, Hannah Margaret (daughter of the Proprietor), 61, 65
Penn, John, 54, 58, 70
Penn, Letitia, 25, 53, 58, 60, 66
Penn, Margaret (sister of the Proprietor), 16
Penn, Margaret (daughter of the Proprietor), 63
Penn, Margaret (Jasper) Vanderschuren (mother of the Proprietor), 4-5, 33
Penn, Mary (Jones), 52-53, 66
Penn, Richard (brother of the Proprietor), 24
Penn, Richard (son of the Proprietor), 64, 70
Penn, Springett, 25, 50, 52
Penn, Thomas, 58, 70
Penn, William (great-great-grandfather of the Proprietor), 2
Penn, William (great-grandfather of the Proprietor), 2
Penn, *Admiral Sir* William, 1-2, 6, 8, 18, 21; acquires Irish estates, 4-6; death, 22; and founding of Pennsylvania, 2, 27; impeachment, 17; imprisonment, 4; knighted, 6; marriage, 4; naval career, 2, 4, 11, 13-14; personality, 5; relations with son, 8-11, 14, 17, 20; relations with Stuarts, 1, 13-14, 26-27, 40; as Royalist, 6, 8
Penn, William (Proprietor of Pennsylvania). Ancestry, 2; birth, 2, 4; and boundary disputes, 27, 29, 33, 35-37, 40; charges of incompetence, 39, 43-44, 52, 54, 58-59; children, 24-26, 33-34, 42, 54, 58, 60-64, 70; death, 70; disputes with colonists, 43-45, 47-48, 50, 56-57, 63, 71; education, 5, 8, 11; finances, 23, 36-37, 42, 44, 48, 50, 53-54, 59-66, 71; health, 34, 49, 54, 58, 67, 69; imprisonment, 16-18, 22, 65-66; and Indians, 30, 35, 37, 55-56; influence of, 1, 25, 32, 49, 71-72; in Ireland, 5, 14, 16; and James II, 13, 24, 26, 29, 33, 39-40, 43-45; at Lincoln's Inn, 11, 13; as manager, 42, 47, 50, 71; marriages, 23, 50; military experience and aspirations, 14, 16; as naval aide, 11, 13; at Oxford, 8-9; personality, 5, 70-71; and Philadelphia, 31-32, 54; politics and government, 1, 11, 24-25, 29, 31-33, 35-37, 39, 43-44, 47, 52, 54-55, 65-66, 71-72; portrait, 14; Proprietor of Pennsylvania, 1-2, 29, 31-32, 36, 40, 50, 53, 59, 61, 66-67, 71; and Quakers, 1, 5, 16-18, 20-23, 25-26, 39, 42, 49, 66; religious disputation, 17-18; suspected of treason, 26, 40, 45, 49; thought of, 1, 9-11, 16-18, 20, 22-23, 26, 33, 43, 49, 52, 55-56, 70-71; visits France, 10-11; visits Germany, 23, 25; visits Holland, 23, 25; visits Pennsylvania (1682), 34-37, 39; visits Pennsylvania (1699), 53-58; writings, 18, 22-23, 30, 49, 52
Penn, William, Jr., 26, 52-53, 62-67, 70
Penn family of Buckinghamshire, 2
Penn-Mead trial, 21-22
Pennsbury, 35, 37, 54-55, 58
Pennsylvania, 1, 25, 50, 58, 61, 64, 67, 70, 72; boundaries, 27, 29, 33, 35-37, 40, 43; Charter, 29-30, 37, 43-44, 48-49, 56, 59, 66; economy, 1, 30, 37, 71; evolution, 1, 71; government, 29-30, 31-33, 35-36, 39, 42, 44, 47, 49-50, 54, 57-58, 66, 69, 71; Indian relations, 37; naming of, 2, 27; pacifism, 30, 37, 39, 47-50, 52, 56, 60, 62; proprietorship of, 1, 29-30, 36; settlement, 30-31, 36
Pepys, Samuel, 9
Philadelphia, 29, 31-32, 35, 39, 48, 53-54, 58, 60, 62, 65
Philadelphia County, 34
Piracy, 39, 43, 52, 54-55

Plague, 13
Pope, The, 18, 23, 26
Prayer Book, Anglican, 9
Presbyterians, 17-18
Primogeniture, 64
Privy Council, 18, 44, 59
Protestants, 2, 4, 21, 23, 26-27, 40, 43-45
Provence, 11
Puritans, 8-9

Quakers, 1, 5, 9-10, 16-17, 20-21, 23-27, 33, 35, 39-40, 45, 49, 54, 56, 59, 61-63, 65, 71
Quary, *Col.* Robert, 55, 58-59, 61, 63
Quitrents, 30, 36-37, 42, 48, 60
Quo Warranto, 40

Religion (see also Catholics, Catholicism; Church of England; "Fifth Monarchists"; Jesuits; Nonconformists; Pope, The; Presbyterians; Protestants; Puritans; Quakers; Trinity, doctrine of the), 1-2, 5, 25-30, 33, 43, 57, 59, 70-71
Revolution of 1688, 44
Rickmansworth, Herts., 23, 25-26
Rotterdam, 11
Royal Society, The, 30
Royalists, 2, 4-6, 8-9
Ruscumbe, Berks., 66-67, 69
Rye, Christopher, 16

St. Omer, 26
Salé, Morocco, 2
Sandy Foundations Shaken, 18
Saumur, 10-11, 26
Scheveningen, 6
Scotch-Irish, 36
Scots, 31
Second Frame of Government, 35-36, 43-44, 47-48
Shackamaxon, 35
Shanagarry, 6, 14, 16, 20, 42
Slavery, Slave Trade, 32, 56
Smuggling, 39, 43, 52, 54-55
Some Account of the Province of

Pennsylvania, 30
Spencer, Robert, 11, 27
Springett, Gulielma Maria. See Penn, Gulielma Maria (Springett)
Starling, *Sir* Samuel, 21-22
Stillingfleet, *Dr.* Edward, 18
Stuart monarchy, 6, 13, 45; gratitude of to Sir William Penn, 1, 13-14, 26-27, 40
Sunderland, Earl of. See Spencer, Robert
Sussex County, Delaware, 35
Sweden, Swedes, 21, 30
Sydney, Algernon, 11, 26, 32

Tamamend, 35
Taxation, 30, 32, 35-37, 48-49, 53, 60
Test Act, 23, 26, 42
Third Frame of Government, 50, 52, 57
"Three Lower Counties," 29, 33, 35, 39, 47, 57, 59, 61
Tower of London, 5, 18
Trinity, doctrine of the, 18
Truth Rescued from Impostors, 22
Turin, 11

Upland, Pa., 34

Venables, *Gen.* Robert, 5
Vincent, Thomas, 17-18

Wales, Welsh, 27, 31, 36
Wanstead, Essex, 4-5, 17
Welcome (bark), 34
West Jersey (see also New Jersey), 24-26, 31, 35
Weymouth, 6, 8
William III, 43-45, 47-48, 50, 58-59
William of Orange. See William III
Worminghurst, Sussex, 25, 42, 50, 53, 63, 65

York, Duke of. See James II
Yorkshire, 16